▪ *Life Without Work*

A time for change, growth and personal transformation

CHRISTINE INGHAM

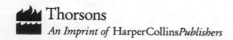

Thorsons
An Imprint of HarperCollins*Publishers*

Thorsons
An Imprint of HarperCollins*Publishers*
77–85 Fulham Palace Road
Hammersmith, London W6 8JB

First published by Thorsons 1994
10 9 8 7 6 5 4 3 2 1

A catalogue record for this book
is available from the British Library

ISBN 0 7225 2931 7

Typeset by Harper Phototypesetters Limited, Northampton
Printed and bound in Great Britain by Mackays of Chatham PLC, Kent

■ Contents

▪ *Introduction*

During the two years or so which I spent unemployed, I must have gone through stages of anguish, despair and worry a hundred times. Money worries; what am I going to do worries; when will it all end worries. But throughout it all I was aware that, although lots of doors seemed to be closing firmly shut, others were opening up. Much soul-searching eventually led me to a gradual understanding of where I really wanted to be — and it wasn't in the direction of career queen. Instead, once I had acknowledged openly my real dream (to write), a whole range of chance encounters and events took me to where I wanted to be, complete with the ideal part-time job to help finance my new beginnings.

For me, being unemployed proved to be the most rewarding time of my life despite being incredibly challenging too, complete with rocketing debts and almost losing my home. But I do believe that the difficulties we are given are there to help us grow, and that we are never given problems that are more than we can cope with. This is so hard to appreciate at first when we are being tested by the new challenges which face us; but just as plants are cut back to help them grow, we too sometimes have our waywardness pruned to help us onto an improved path for growth. *Life Without Work* is written out of these convictions, with the aim of showing the more positive aspects of unemployment, while giving suggestions as to how to deal with the negative ones.

The book also aims to give an element of that sparse commodity: hope. For many this has all but disappeared in the face of severe recruitment practices and contraction of the labour market. The recession has only made matters worse. Full and secure employment as we have previously known it may now be a thing of the past, along with unemployment figures in the thousands instead of millions. To jump ahead of the game, learn the rules and play by them instead of against them, whilst bending them to suit our own aims, is the only sensible way forward. Clinging to old ideals holds us back, but seeing the opportunities in the new forms which are emerging offers new possibilities. Although this is not a book about how to get a job (there are plenty of those type of books available on the market), I hope it helps to identify some of those new possibilities for ways in which to work, including making your own.

Becoming and being unemployed can be seen as the end of your personal world, or as a challenge and a wonderful opportunity to reassess one's life and shape it into something infinitely more fulfilling. It's an opportunity to re-design your way of being in the world and a challenge to find out what the experience has to teach you. Without addressing the issues which are presented to us we leave ourselves open and vulnerable should the same thing happen again at a later date. I hope this book provides some ideas as to how you can meet these challenges and start to build a more secure future for yourself.

There are chapters on looking after one's physical and mental health during unemployment — things which can too easily be overlooked while worrying over more immediate concerns. Family and personal relationships are also addressed, including a look at what the non-unemployed person can do to help. A separate chapter addresses people who live on their own and looks at some of the particular issues that may affect them.

A life without work can seem like a gloomy prospect, no matter how temporary it may be and regardless of whether you are experiencing it because of redundancy, disability, job shortage or retirement. But it can also be a time, unfettered from the shackles of a job, to explore your own rich potential; to listen to the quiet voice of calm, your intuition, your true self whose whispers about the way to find a more fulfilling life may have gone unheard for too long amid the jumble and clatter of work, work, work. While you read, listen to what that voice is saying. Listen to the truths it wants to tell you.

1 ▪ *An Opportunity for Reassessment*

It can be the worst of times; but the good news is, it can also be the best of times. Challenging it definitely is. From experience I'm only too aware of the difficulties which present themselves during a period of unemployment. After returning from nine months travelling I had little to help me settle back into life other than a very large overdraft. And it was getting bigger. Life went downhill from there — for a while, until I began to see that although being without work was presenting severe problems, it was also presenting some wonderful opportunities. The trick, I realized, was in opening my eyes so that I could begin to see those opportunities when they presented themselves to me, grab hold of them, and start to use them. Opportunity disguised as loss might be one way of looking at being unemployed.

As individuals we are experiencing the result of what is happening on a more global scale. It would seem that whilst the economies in industrialized countries still rattle their way along based on consumerism and the hunt for profit, mass unemployment is bound to remain a feature of modern life. After all, Jo Public can buy only so many video recorders/washing machines/computers. So, as demand decreases and the boss looks for more ways in which to cut overheads, more people find themselves out of work. It seems that unemployment is here to stay, at least for the foreseeable future, and not only in this country but in other developed nations across the globe.

But we are not without power in this situation. Consider the uses of adversity. Consider for a moment the gift you have been given through being unemployed: Time. This is the one thing you have now been provided with — for free. For the moment you have this wonderful breathing space in which to stand back calmly and have a good, long, hard look at just what is, and has, been going on in your life, and more importantly just where you want it to go in the future. Whether you have been made redundant, have just retired, appear to have limited prospects of employment because of a disability, have specific constraints with which you have to cope, or that you are young and have not had a job up to now, this is a period in your life which is here to present you with an opportunity to reflect on 'What it's all about.' You may never have this time again.

Think back to a period in your life when your time was spoken for; perhaps at school or in your last job. There may have been many times when you thought longingly of the time to come, perhaps over a holiday period, when your time would be your own. Or imagine meeting an old friend who bemoans the fact that their job is eating their life away, and imagine the envy with which they walk away after listening to you talk of the time you do have. And remember those times when your body took refuge in illnesses to give you a much needed break from the unending daily toil.

So why doesn't this time you have been given seem so sweet? Perhaps because anything in excess suddenly seems to lose its appeal. One cream cake is delicious, especially if they have been restricted because of being on a diet. Twelve cream cakes in an hour, with more to come, suddenly becomes a very unappetizing proposition. So too with what seems to be an unending supply of days. I remember at one point on my twenty-first birthday, normally a time for celebration, feeling very miserable indeed. I was in my final year at college and I suddenly realized that on completing the year I would no longer have any more convenient two- or three-year academic stints to guide me, as had been the case to date with school and college. The next visible sign-post I could see was some sixty years down the line to retirement. I sobbed. I should have realized then that my heart was trying to tell me something. Namely, that the prospect of being employed by someone for that length of time was not what was going to bring me joy. Instead it took me many years of work before I learned to listen properly to what I already seemed to know deep inside.

In actual fact the sixty years was soon broken down into smaller, more manageable portions: two years in one job, three years in another, and then promotion for another few years etc. It all became much easier to handle once I realized this. In the same way, the time you have now can also be broken down into more manageable units. Decide that instead of this unending time stretching out into who knows where, you have only the next six months without paid work. In reality you might have less than that. If you are job hunting you may be offered something tomorrow, and with hindsight you might then find yourself wanting this time over again! What fickle creatures we are — and how easy it is to see things clearly from the vantage point of experience.

So think in terms of only the next six months. Assume that you will be unemployed until then (although you might not be). Look at the time now as having a limit to it. Hopefully it will help take away the anxiety which surrounds not knowing. Being unsure of when it will all end can be paralysing and depressing, so tell yourself how long you do have and feel the difference in how you now look at the future. It suddenly becomes manageable, and of a size you can do something with. If you feel three months would be better for you, then give yourself three months, or however long you feel happy with. At the end of six months you might need to give yourself another six, but at least the overlong year has been broken down into more manageable parts.

Failure to accept your situation can also be another block to moving successfully forward through this period. It is very easy to blame others for your situation, saying it was the fault of bad management, the Government, or cheaper foreign imports. The thing is that blaming anyone for what has happened (including yourself if you have been self-employed) doesn't really help. It only serves to keep you stuck at the point where things began to change, and loses you a lot of energy as you sit there stewing in frustration. You can instead accept where you are right now. No blame, just an acceptance. You are here, right now, and you are unemployed. Now who is going to do something about it? It would be nice to think that someone else is, but at the end of the day the only person who can take your life forward from here is you. You could try sitting around and waiting for the pound to rise, the Dm to do nice things or the dollar to work wonders so that industry is boosted and people come knocking on your door with offers of work; but let's face it, that could be a long wait. Instead, this situation you are in is now your own special responsibility for you to handle. In accepting that responsibility you are able to regain a sense of control over your life and feel empowered. You no longer have to feel that you are the victim of some remote person's business decisions. You are the person who makes the decisions about your life and how you want it to go from now on. And the best way to succeed at doing that is to listen to, and follow, your heart.

This time has been given to you as an opportunity; an opportunity to change and grow as you meet the challenge to find out just what form the opportunity is taking for you. At the very least it is a chance to learn how to build a new life which is less dependent on employment for a sense of security. Even if you found another job tomorrow, most people now realize that it would be no guarantee that unemployment will not happen again in the future. The chance you have now is to build for yourself a sort of insurance policy; one which is strong enough to withstand the vagaries of any boss, economic situation or other outside force.

▪ YOUR CAREER

Losing your job or being without work can be a good time to reassess what you have been working at or aiming for up to now. It is an opportunity to stand back and see if this time has been given to you as a chance perhaps to change track, or even to find out what track you should really have been on in the first place.

It is convenient for us to think of ourselves as A Solicitor, A Shop Assistant or A Steel Worker. We do the job well and therefore define ourselves in that way. You go to a party and the new person you've just been introduced to inevitably asks the question 'And what do you do?' 'I'm a bank clerk', you reply. So what happens when the job goes and someone asks the same question? Some continue to define themselves in the same way, others mumble 'I'm unemployed' (although thankfully, being unemployed is losing its stigma as it becomes more common). It seems that we either limit our potential by continuing to see ourselves in the same restricted light, or we almost cease to exist when the job ceases. This is where the real dangers of being unemployed lie. Linking our sense of self with a job which we do in the main for money's sake. No job = no self. Ouch!

Work is important. It brings lots of benefits with it besides the wage packet: sense of purpose and direction, companionship, meaningful use of time. But without the pay packet, I wonder how many would return to their job as a solicitor/shop assistant/steel worker. I also wonder what other hidden talents lie dormant while we stick these job titles on our introductions.

Now is an opportunity to redefine yourself, to investigate all your other possible 'You's' and perhaps invent a new reality for yourself. You can do this is in one of two ways: by undergoing formal career analysis, or by following a more intuitive approach.

Formal Career/Job Analysis

There are a number of formal ways in which you can get help in trying to find out about which careers would suit you. Your local Careers Service, which caters mainly for school leavers, may also have facilities for giving advice to adults. They might be your first port of call. It will probably help to go along with some idea of the type of job you might be interested in or the specific fields that interest you. They will advise you about suitable careers, including details of any qualifications you might need beforehand and how you might go about getting them.

If you really don't have a clue what you want to do, perhaps because you've always been a bank clerk and don't know of any other jobs, or because you realize that your last jobs haven't been what you've really wanted, then more in-depth work needs to be done. They may have facilities to help you find your direction, in the form of computer programmes, videos, assessment tests, or books, so do ask.

If these facilities aren't available in your area you could approach any professional organizations of which you may be a member. For example, the Institute of Management offers career counselling at a reduced price to its members as well as to non-member professionals. There are also commercial organizations which offer in-depth career analysis to help assess your skills and abilities and identify possible career options which might be open to you. They can be a little expensive to use, but if you have redundancy pay, you might want to think of using it to help you identify new potential careers for you. Although you will obviously be very conscious about money, spending some on this might well be an investment in the long term. But do assess carefully what they have to offer, and ask if they have people whom you can talk to who have used their services. Local provision is advertised in Yellow Pages.

Institute of Management
Management House
Cottingham Road
Corby
Northants NN17 1TT
Tel. 0536 204222

Without access to funds, there are still ways in which you can investigate new directions. Take a trip to your local library, or if it isn't a very large one, your nearest central or main library. Browse through the books in the careers section to give you some ideas. There are lots of books available, not only for school leavers, but also for career changers. They may also have a different selection of books in their reference section.

If nothing appeals to you from the selection available, a little bit of self-assessment might help. We tend only to look for jobs that match our paper qualifications. We overlook the fact that we have other marketable qualities which can also provide a good foundation for a career.

Spend some time thinking about:

- Knowledge

  What do you know about? What could you talk about at length if someone asked you to? It might be knowledge you've acquired through your reading interests, television viewing, hobbies, your upbringing, your culture etc. Think about things other than just what you might have studied formally.

- Experience

  Think about the experience you have gained up to now in life, in a very broad sense. As a teenager you might think you have none other than signing on and facing the realities of unemployment. That is still a valuable experience and, if you reflect on it, has probably taught you one or two things, if only patience in the face of benefit interviews. So think about the experience you have gained in life both in and outside of work, both good and bad.

- Skills

  Again, we tend to concentrate only on the specific skills we have learned as part of a job. We have many other life skills which are also very marketable, for example communication skills, listening skills, craft skills, how to sail a boat etc. Consider the many different aspects of your life, all the different roles you play throughout the day, and list the skills you have which help you play each one.

• Abilities and aptitudes
Where do your natural abilities lie? Perhaps in sports, in handling people, or with the written word. What do you seem to find it easy to learn about, or easy to do, almost without thinking? You might be a practical person, or someone who finds mental pursuits a doddle.

Assessing yourself in this way can give some real insights into what sort of career you might best be suited to. Doing it on your own can be quite difficult, though, because we tend to see ourselves in one way and overlook our other special abilities. Enlist the help of friends or family who can be rather more objective about your talents. Explain to them what you are trying to do, and that it is the positive feedback you're interested in.

An Intuitive Approach

Undertaking a structured career analysis might well suggest to you the field you would best be working in, or at the very least confirm what you already suspected. However, although a useful exercise, it might still not come up with any answers you feel are right. A valid and logical suggestion may have been made in terms of making use of your many talents, but you may feel uninspired by it. Or it could be that you aren't in a position to go to a careers analyst or seek professional help. There is another way forward, which relies on your own inner knowledge.

It is worth asking yourself whether you would do a suggested job for free. For example, if they offered you your old job back, would you do it for no pay? If the next employer you applied to said yes, they wanted you but no, they couldn't pay wages, would you do it? Working just for money alone rarely brings lasting happiness. It might temporarily solve a few immediate problems, but in the long term job satisfaction cannot be yours. Instead, the job-for-money proves to be a strait-jacket, preventing you from finding your life's true purpose and meaning.

However, working at what you love doing, at that which your heart tells you to do, will not only bring happiness and success but also the money you need. Doing work which your head tells you you have to, or because your ego tells you it must do from greed, for money, or for status will not lead to a happy work situation, no matter what. And if you're not happy, ultimately you won't do well in life.

We spend so much of our lives at work that I feel we owe it to ourselves to make sure that we are doing what we really want to do, rather than what we have to. Now is a time to clarify the fulfilment you would like from a job, the enjoyment you want to feel each work-day, the enrichment you want it to give to your life. A careers analyst might come up with the answer, but the answer already lies within you. Ask anyone what their dream job is and you have the basis for their new career. So, you might say you want to be Prime Minister. Think about what elements there are to that job which really appeal and you can start to realize which field you would be happiest working in. Go ahead. Ask yourself what your dream job is; that which has perhaps always been there in the quiet, secret, heart of you. What enthuses you? What do you get excited about? What gives you energy when you do it? If you feel a slump in the heart when you think of doing certain jobs, perhaps your last one, then you might do well to think of other areas in which you might work. A successful career, lies in doing the things which excite us and give us genuine pleasure.

Following your dream is completely different from letting a job give you your identity, like the bank clerk who feels s/he doesn't exist when the job goes. The job has been like a bolt on identity, covering the space where a true sense of identity should be. In contrast, when we work at something that seems to come from within, we only serve to enhance our real sense of self.

Perhaps you don't think you have a dream tucked away, waiting for its chance to come. In which case, simply ask yourself what it is you want to do. That's all you have to do. Ask the question and then leave the issue alone for the answer to come to you. It's a bit like when you're trying to solve a cross-word puzzle or remember the name of that famous film star. You sit and ponder directly for hours. Nothing. Then when you leave it alone, perhaps to go and make a cup of tea or to pick the children up from school, PING!, the answer comes straight to mind completely unaided and when your mind is on something else. It's the same with finding your way into the work that is for you. Simply ask, and the answer will eventually be given.

When you are doing what is right for you, you will feel that work has become like play because you enjoy it so much. That's not to say that it will not present challenges any more. It will. But as Andrew Ferguson says in his book *Creating Abundance*, work is the best 'personal growth workshop'. It is there to teach you about yourself, if you can learn to see the personal lessons involved.

This time which you have available now is a time for discovery. It is an opportunity to create a marriage between your own inner hopes and dreams and your outer reality so that you need not have to accept low-paid work or work with low satisfaction levels again — unless you choose to in order to help you reach your dream (much like actors who work as cleaners because it keeps them going financially until they get the job they want). Use this time wisely. Use it to reassess where you are going, and what you want out of your life because, who knows, you may not have this chance for reflection again for a long time to come.

This will obviously be a time when you find yourself having to reassess your financial situation. It's best to do this as soon as you can. You might have the cushion of redundancy pay or a few weeks' wages in hand, tempting you to carry on spending as normal. Acting in this way is part of the mechanism which we use to limit the full impact of staring the unemployment situation full in the face and accepting that there may not be a wage coming in for the next few months, at least. But the sooner the horns are drawn in, the better. If not, debts will start to accumulate faster than you thought.

So, as with any new enterprise (and you could look on being unemployed as a new venture), you need to draw up a cash flow. This can sound daunting when talked about in hushed tones by bank managers and the like, but all you need to do is:

- Take a large sheet of paper.
- Divide it up into twelve columns — one for each month.
- Column 1 is the month you are in now.
- Write down the bills you will have to pay in each month.
  It might take you some time to remember ALL the things you pay for throughout the year. Include amounts for housekeeping.
- Write down the income you will have for each month.
- Add up the bills for each month.
- Take this away from the income.
- The difference will show you where the difficulties lie.

This might be the point when you start taking sidelong glances at the family silver and wondering where the nearest pawn-broker is. Before you do, think of what else a new enterprise does besides drawing up a cash flow. It also exercises budgetary controls to keep an eye on overheads and make sure money isn't being wasted unnecessarily.

You can look at this next activity with a furrowed brow and pained expression — or you can look on it with a sense of fun (or a challenge, for the Type A personalities among you). If you have a family, do include them in this. Not only might the kids come up with some wacky ideas which might also prove workable, but it's important for them to feel included in the decision-making process since paring down the budget is going to affect them too. They'll understand better if later on they have an ardent request for a treat turned down with a firm 'No'.

Set everyone tasks eg to come up with three ways to save money on lunches; six ways to save money on heating costs; find ten ways of giving treats that don't cost anything. Give everyone a few days to report back to another house meeting. Listen to everyone's ideas, write them down and consider each one in turn. Keep the whole thing dynamic, giving people new challenges each week and working out a reward system.

Extend the concept of the six-month rule which you applied earlier to your thinking in the previous chapter. Or perhaps a twelve-month plan with agreements to have three-monthly reviews. Giving target dates which are not too far distant helps everyone feel that the restraints are not forever. Nothing is.

So, to get a good overall picture of your personal or family budget, first list all the minutiae of where the monies go — then evaluate where each penny is spent. Ask whether each item is necessary, like really, really necessary? Everyone will believe that their little bit of spending is absolutely sacrosanct. OK. Let it go for the first round. Pick off the easy things first. Then go for a second, third, fourth, or as many rounds as it takes to trim the budget down until it fits into the new (temporary) scheme of things. Placate mutinous uprisings with reminders of the review in three months' time. And do remember to include a budget for small treats. None of us minds having to be frugal so long as we are rewarded for our efforts. You might like to build up a list of free treats to give, using that list of ten suggestions someone came up with as a start. Making a list of treats which cost nothing (or very little) is a useful, ongoing exercise to help focus on the important things in life which give real joy, like a hug, doing someone a good turn, telling someone how much you love them.

If you find that things really won't balance, don't panic:

- Contact your local Citizen's Advice Bureau. They will help you work out what action to take, such as mortgage deferment and rescheduling of debts.
- Go to your library for books on handling debt and cash crises, such as *Get Out of Debt and Prosper* by Peter Cutler (Thorsons, 1991).
- Contact the National Debtline on 021 359 8501.
- Read on.

National Debtline
Tel. 021 359 8501

After staring at figures and doing the basic money work, now might be a good opportunity to reflect more broadly on what money really is all about. What place does it have in your life? What meaning does it hold? These might seem silly questions, with the inevitable cry of 'Well, you're not much good without it.' But being in a position now where you are probably experiencing a lack of it, consider for a moment what you are being offered to learn.

We are used to thinking that money is something to have, to acquire, to get more of. But money does not equal happiness. Neither do the possessions which it can buy. Nothing which is outside of ourselves can give us true happiness, regardless of whether it is a new car, a beautiful house, or an enviable wardrobe of clothes. Things like that may give a temporary shot in the arm, an amusing lift, but inevitably we tire of them because they go out of fashion, lose their value or a new and better model comes along. Suddenly the thing we desired so much doesn't satisfy us any more. Or it might be that your possessions are stolen, lost, or broken. How dangerous a position to be in if your only chance of happiness rested with that special object which has now forever disappeared from your life. Does this mean you no longer have a chance to be happy? No. Real and lasting happiness is something which is within us. True happiness is right there already, waiting to be coaxed out. (See Chapter 6). You don't need to think about its costly upkeep or worry about trading it in for a new model. Neither can it be stolen from you — although at the moment it might be a bit lost.

Not having much money provides us with an opportunity to learn how to find the true value in things. It's a bit like the twelve cream cakes again. They suddenly lose their value when presented ad infinitum yet become objects to write home about when scarce.

Imagine for a moment a freak point in time where money has become utterly worthless, much like it did in the Wall Street crash. Imagine the absolute despair you would feel at the time you had wasted in trying to accumulate as much of it as possible. You would think of the sacrifices you had made, the life you had led, the real opportunities you had missed. How would you have spent your life differently if you had known this would happen? What would you see as having real value?

Perhaps the mid-life crisis is a bit like a personal Wall Street. You're old enough by this time to have acquired a lot of things and perhaps satisfied many of the material cravings of the outer world. You're mature enough, and in a position to stand back and ask 'But what else is there?' Being unemployed provides a short-cut to getting to that same question. Suddenly you are forced to look at money and material possessions and evaluate things anew.

If you have identified yourself too closely with your job, or believe you are a non-person without one, inevitably your self-esteem disappears along with the prospect of work. This is also reflected through money. Money and self are inextricably linked. With a shaky self-esteem, if money goes your sense of personal worth can seem to go, too. It's common for people to experience a lack of money as a lack of self in some way, as though they are no longer of value in other people's eyes. But if money is so closely linked with self-esteem or other emotions in this way, can we turn that knowledge to our advantage?

New thinking about prosperity and abundance would say 'Yes'. Whatever we are on the inside (emotions, beliefs, etc), forms our experience of outer reality. For example, through being unemployed I became heavily in debt. In having to focus on the issue very closely I came to realize that money had in fact always been a difficulty for me. I also came to realize how my emotions and beliefs were being reflected in how money manifested itself throughout my life. I had always felt that I was carrying around an emotional overdraft: too many outgoings and not enough incoming. Eventually it dawned on me that the actual overdraft in the bank was reflecting an inner feeling of being emotionally bankrupt. The change in fortunes happened with a change within me. Sorting through the emotional issues led to an eventual increase in positive feelings — and a positive cash flow for the first time ever! Note the way round it happened. Only *after* I had sorted out myself on the inside did an improvement in the money situation on the outside take place.

You could think of debt and money problems as being like an illness. Treating the symptoms might bring a temporary relief: if I had rescheduled my debts it would have helped for the time being, but as sure as ECUs are ECUs, the same old problems would have arisen again at some other time. So try to get to the root of your own difficulties. Ask, 'What lesson do I need to learn now? What is going on in me to create this?' It might be that your money situation is making you stop for a while. Consider why. Accept it and work with it and make it your new goal to endeavour to learn as much as you can from the opportunity.

Hamlet could have been talking about money when he said, 'There is nothing, either good or bad, but thinking makes it so.' Money isn't good and neither is it bad. It is more like a sort of energy and when we clear all our difficult and blocking emotions within, we create a path for a free flow of all energy in our lives, including one for money. Just think of how physically drained you feel when you become worried or depressed about something. Negative emotions *block*. Everything seems to go wrong and no positive things seem to be able to find their way into your life. So too with money. Its chameleon-like properties merely become part of your present experience. If you're feeling negative, money will not be a source of joy for you.

All this makes very good news. To improve your experience of money, simply improve what is going on within you. To make it easier for your cash flow to become sorted, stay focused on your life goals. You will soon find out if they are appropriate goals by the success you will experience in your needs being met. If your goal is in reality only a shallow, materialistic one then the route to funding it will be a struggle. If it is one which is in tune with your true inner needs then you might be pleasantly surprised at the help you suddenly receive. Let your needs be known as you did with asking for career/life direction. Go inside yourself and ask that your needs be met, and then just trust. Try not to worry about the outcome; it will only create an unnecessary block. Someone I knew was very good at all this. She would fund a project from nothing, having complete trust that the money would be there when she needed it. Without savings or rich uncles in the background, she was always proved right. So ask, trust and then forget about it.

• INCOME WHILE UNEMPLOYED

Being on Unemployment Benefit or Income Support means that money is excruciatingly tight. Opportunities to earn a little more on the side without it affecting your benefit are few, but they do exist.

If you are claiming Unemployment Benefit:

- You can earn up to £2 a day, Monday to Saturday inclusive, in addition to your benefit.
- On Sundays you can take your weekly earnings up to £56 without it affecting your benefit. £56 or more and you will lose all your Unemployment Benefit.
- In both cases you can only work less than 16 hours; 16 hours or more a week and you lose your benefit.
- The amount you earn is what you take home after tax, NI, and other expenses have been taken off which allow you to do the job, including fares to and from work.
- Your employer can, in addition to the cash you receive, pay you in kind with, for example, cigarettes, meals, food, luncheon vouchers without it affecting your benefit.

If you are claiming Income Support you mustn't work 16 hours or more, but bearing this in mind:

- You and your partner can both earn up to £5 a week each to top up your benefit. Anything over that is taken off, £ for £, from your benefit.
- The Sunday rule doesn't apply if you are on Income Support.
- If you and your partner are under 60 and have both been receiving Income Support for more than two years, you are allowed to earn £15 a week between you.
- If you or your partner are members of the Territorial Army, the Reserve Force, a lifeboat crew (or launch or staff one), are an auxiliary coastguard or a part-time fire fighter you can also earn up to £15 a week. If you don't earn as much as this from your duties, you or your partner can earn up to another £5 from other work as well, up to a maximum of £15.
- You can keep two thirds of any income from child-minding. After taking off expenses and the amount you are allowed to earn (ie £5 or £15), the remaining third is taken off, £ for £, from your benefit.

- You can also take in lodgers (a lodger is someone you prepare at least one meal a day for) and keep the first £20 of the rent you receive plus half of the rest.
- You can keep all of the payment you receive from acting as an occasional foster parent.
- You can receive £10 a week on a regular basis from a charity without it affecting your benefit.
- You can receive irregular payments from charities so long as it doesn't take your savings over £3000. Anything above this is taken off, £ for £, from your benefit. There are a multitude of charities up and down the country which have funds available for things like holidays, clothing, debt repayment and many other things. It is well worth looking into. If the money is there, and you fulfil their criteria, then go ahead and apply. Someone will receive their money and it may as well be you. Go to the library and spend some time going through *A Guide to Grants for Individuals in Need*, published by the Directory of Social Change.
- You are also allowed payments from someone else to a third party so long as the payment isn't in exchange for work and isn't for the essentials which Income Support is supposed to pay for, like food, heating, clothing and accommodation costs. If some kindly person offered to pay off your credit card bill, for example, or some other outstanding debt, this would not affect your benefit at all.

So, taken all together there is some scope for improving your income while you are having to claim benefit. I know £5 a week doesn't sound much, but it amounts to some £260 over the year. Of course they make it difficult for you and won't like it if you earn the money from the same regular part-time job throughout the year, but if in doubt, contact your local Citizens' Advice Bureau or dial the Freephone Benefits Helpline on 0800 666555.

The list above is not totally comprehensive. There are many special allowances, for example if you have a disability, or are a single parent, or are retired. If you think you might be a

```
┌──────────────────────────────────────────────────┐
│              Freephone Benefits Helpline           │
│              Tel. 0800 666555                      │
└──────────────────────────────────────────────────┘
```

special case, do check with the places mentioned above.

▪ ACCOMMODATION

In looking at your finances and ways in which overheads can be reduced, where you live might offer some things to consider:

- How important is it to live where you do? Could you move to a cheaper area? Do some research on the possibilities to help you weigh up the pros and cons.
- If you own where you live, could you sell it to release some of the capital?
- What about living abroad? Living in a quiet little cottage in Ireland for a while might give you the break and the breathing space you need to reassess the turn your life is taking and help you decide which direction you would like it to take in order to bring it more fully in line with your true life goal.
- Consider ways in which you can make your home earn money for you, eg letting, hiring to film crews, converting your garage into a space to let.
- Consider building your own home, as a group of unemployed people did in Tyneside.

▪ CAPITALIZING ON THE REASSESSMENT

Holding the magnifying glass up to the many aspects of your life which you may have taken for granted for some time should highlight areas for change. Taking nothing for granted any more and seeing your everyday life anew allows for new insights to take place: you may be on benefit and your movements appear restricted, but there *is* room for progress; your career seems to have been blocked, but yet there are new paths open to investigation; your lifestyle seemed fixed by immutable laws and yet, yes, there are ways to meet the challenge of changing it for something different but equally or even more exciting (what *would* it be like to have a film crew take over your home for £1000 a day?).

Every bit of research you carry out, every new thing you discover, each new proposition you consider, presents new opportunities. Each change you put into action is a challenge, perhaps bringing with it new skills and experiences. Be aware of all the new things you are learning and always be asking yourself if there is anything you could use to add to your CV.

Your research into releasing the potential in your home could have unearthed some surprising possibilities — how could you make that knowledge work for you? In looking at how to reduce living expenses you might have had the passing thought that someone ought to design a more cost-effective appliance — could that person be you? Or in reassessing your career you might have developed some insights into how best to go about doing it — could you capitalize on this?

At every turn we are given new chances. Being unemployed presents a multitude. The trick is in learning how to spot them.

3 ▪ On the Work Front

Job hunting can become a job in itself. It can also become pretty soul destroying after a while, especially if it is the main activity on which all else hangs. I hope Chapter 1 will have set you thinking about finding a job which is more 'you'. If you already know what it is, then the hard work is done and things will start to move forward for you, as recently happened with my nephew. He has been unemployed for some time, trying to get into wig making which he thought was just the job for him. The way has been blocked for him at every turn, but he has just written to me saying that he has suddenly been offered help by some people to become a professional body piercer (beautifying the body with jewellery). This has been one of his interests for a very long time but he had obviously been overlooking the possibility of it holding his future until it was, almost literally, put under his nose for him. Now it looks like he is eventually going to be running his own business. All of us are being guided and offered help like this towards realizing our true selves all the time — but we have to keep an eye open for it. And when it does come along, you will instinctively know — it will just feel right and your gut reaction will give you a resounding 'Yes'.

But in the meantime, there is still the pressure to look for work, work, work. Perhaps it might be worthwhile taking a second to have a look at what work means to you. You will probably say 'Money' because this assumes a greater importance when you're unemployed and without it, but work also allows us to:

- Feel useful and wanted.
- Meet people and make friends.
- Feel that life has a purpose.
- Practice our learned skills and put our knowledge to use.

However, work is not the only provider of these things. Many other activities offer those same opportunities, as the rest of the book will show.

'But I've still got to have money, to take me from now to the point when I can reach my goal, or even find out what my goal is', you might wail. Think for a moment about people in the arts. You can find actors working in restaurants, artists working as bike couriers and writers as teachers. Ask any of them what they do and they will reply 'I'm an actor/artist/writer.' It is possible for you to operate in the same way. You might know what job or what goal you are aiming for, but in the meantime you need some money. Look on the opportunities to do other sorts of work not as replacing the work you want to do, but as something which still has lots of benefits, such as:

- Providing you with enlightening new experiences.
- Enabling you to meet new people.
- Getting you out of the log-jam of 'I can't get what I want, and so I am stuck, powerless, can do nothing and can't move forward.'

Doing work that you would not normally do becomes less of a trial if:

- You have it clearly set in your mind *why* you are doing it; for example the actor does it to pay the rent while s/he is resting.
- You have in your mind how long you will do it for. This gives you a point in time to work towards when you can re-assess the situation. Nothing is forever.
- You have the attitude that whatever job you do, you are the boss of what you are doing. Act as if the temporary job were your own business and mini-enterprise. It will help to remind you that you are doing it for yourself and your own benefit, so make the job as enjoyable for yourself as you can.
- You consider yourself as having skills which an employer is willing to pay you for. You have something they want. This is just the same as consultants, so think of your make-do job as being like a consultant's short-term contract for work.

The following suggestions for alternative types of work will, I hope, provide a springboard for some ideas of your own. The list is not meant to be comprehensive, and you can tailor the suggestions towards the fields you know, the area you live, your own interests . . . and how desperate you are for money. They are not necessarily meant as a long-term solution, but it is worth bearing in mind that, with an eye on the future, it may be that full employment in the nine-to-five way has seen its day. If you have been made redundant you may have the worry in the back of your mind that it might happen again. One way to insure against this is to have a collection of jobs and different ways in which to generate an income. In this way you can feel more at ease knowing that losing one 10-hour-a-week job from your collection will not be as devastating as losing the one and only 38-hour-a-week job in your life. Flexibility is going to be your best asset, both now and in the future.

▪ PART-TIME WORK

It may seem rather daunting just how many part-time instead of full-time jobs there are. In Britain, the increase may be due to cost-cutting measures on the part of employers who can save more in National Insurance contributions by employing three part-time people at £66 a week (costing them just under £9.18 a week in total) rather than employing one person at £200 a week (which would cost them £20.85). You'll be pleased to know that this anomaly in part-time employment works in your favour, too. You will have to pay £9.62 a week in National Insurance for a job that pays £150, but you don't have to pay anything if you have three jobs at £50 a week — a saving of £500.24 a year, and what a nice holiday that would pay for.

You can also make part-time jobs work in your favour in other ways. If you want to stay on benefit, you can use part-time work to allow you to top up your income (see page 25). Alternatively you could also build up a collection of a few part-time jobs to form a work base until you get the job you want. None of them might be what you ideally want, but in small doses the wide variety could make the novelty of the work-package idea tolerable, if not downright enjoyable.

For example, if you needed an income of, say, £8000 a year it could be made up from a number of unskilled part-time jobs paying, say, £3.25 an hour:

- Two day-time jobs of 15 hours each, perhaps working in a supermarket: £97.50.
- A Sunday job, perhaps working on a Sunday market stall: £25—30.
- A few hours working in the evenings in your favourite pub or restaurant: £21—26.

The work might lead onto full-time employment, or by meeting so many new faces you might get to hear of something else. It's worth remembering that the majority of job vacancies are filled in this way rather than through advertisements.

Contemplating a single part-time job which forfeits your entitlement to benefits is obviously unwise, but there is a lot of potential to be exploited in taking a mix and match approach and developing a package of lots of different jobs.

▪ CASUAL WORK

Many employers, keen to cut overheads, decide to take on staff only when work can be guaranteed. Although Christmas and holiday periods are obvious times for some businesses, others recruit when they have a large, temporary workload, like harvest time on farms. As with part-time work, a one-off job will be of little use if it means loss of benefits, but a whole range of casual work streaming throughout the year could provide you with an opportunity for tremendous variety — and lots of enjoyment.

Keep your eyes open for ads in local papers, shop windows and on business premises. Also contact potential businesses direct and ask to be put on their casual work register. Build up a catalogue of places that have casual work so that you have a pool which you can dip into whenever you need the work flow replenishing. You might be able to use previous work contacts, too. For example, if you know your last employer always had a glut of mailing work to be done twice a year, you could arrange to help out at those times. Competition may be fierce though for some regular casual work such as on farms where you will also be up against the young, fit student population.

Here are some examples you could mix and match from: shops and stores, pubs, entertainment venues, hotels, conference suites, farms, town halls, market research companies, mini-cab driving, product promotions, leaflet distribution, market stalls, factories, odd-jobbing, consultancy work, office work.

▪ JOB SHARING

This form of working has appeal to lots of people who would like to remain in their chosen career but may want to reduce the hours they work. Many large companies operate job-sharing schemes and this may be one way for you to increase your chances of employment. You might not be able to find a suitable full-time job, but you might be able to fit in with someone, perhaps in a post already, who is looking to reduce their hours.

A job-share on its own may not bring in enough to keep your financial wheels oiled, but you can use this as a base around which to structure other job activities such as part-time or casual work.

Write to local employers to enquire whether they operate a job-share scheme, and if so whether they could send you details. If you live in London or the Home Counties, New Ways to Work keeps a job-share register which you can join and which matches people who are looking for similar work. However, they are not an employment agency. Job-sharers make joint applications for vacancies which they have identified themselves. You could ask your local Job Centre if you could advertise on their boards for a partner. Two job-hunters might do better than one.

New Ways to Work
309 Upper Street
London N1 2TU
Tel. 071 226 4026

· RESIDENTIAL WORK

Live-in work has the benefits of cutting down on expensive accommodation costs. The wages are also much lower to take this into account, but residential work might still be an alternative option worth considering. If you own your own home, taking up residential work whilst renting out your own place might be a possibility.

Here are some examples: nannying, social work, companion for an elderly person, domestic help at boarding schools, hotel work, holiday camps, home helps, nursing homes, farms, colleges. Think about what nearby areas have to offer, and also consider the opportunity to live in a different part of the country for a while.

Contacts: your local Social Services department; *The Lady*, *Horse and Hound* and *Nursery World* magazines; *Times Educational Supplement*; local Farmers' Union; Job Centres.

· WORKING ABROAD

Being unemployed on a damp day in Grimsby somehow seems much worse than being unemployed on a sun-soaked beach in Spain. Thanks to the EC, it is now possible to seek work in the rest of the Community, and have your unemployment benefit (but not Income Support) transferred for three months, so long as you are actually looking for work. Sounds appealing, doesn't it? But before you brush the dust off your passport, remember that unemployment is not just a British phenomenon, and zipping off to another country without proper preparation could leave you disillusioned and worse off than before. Contact your local Job Centre for their range of brochures on living and working in each of the other EC countries. They are also starting to carry details of job vacancies abroad. Your local Careers Office also has Euro information available.

Professionals may find the prospect of working abroad, normally on a contract basis, particularly appealing. Management skills can be extremely marketable, especially in developing countries. And unlike Britain, age is considered a positive bonus in some countries. To find work at this level:

- Approach international companies direct.
- Contact management recruitment agencies and consultants (addresses in Yellow Pages).
- Go to your local reference library and ask for a copy of the CEPEC Recruitment Guide which lists agencies and search consultants, many of which handle overseas appointments.
- Consult relevant trade journals, professional associations etc.
- Foreign embassies have copies of their national newspapers which may also carry job vacancies.

If you have experience, but lack formal qualifications to back up applications for jobs in the EC, you may be able to get a Certificate of Experience. It covers a limited number of occupations, but contact the Internal Policy Division of the Department of Trade and Industry for further information.

Internal Policy Division
Department of Trade and Industry
Ashdown House
Victoria Street
London SW1
Tel. 071 215 5610

If you are without qualifications or experience, the prospect of working abroad might inspire you to acquire some marketable skills, especially for less permanent work abroad. There are some which always seem to be in demand:

- Teaching English as a Foreign Language
- Cook/chef
- Sailing certificate
- Nursing
- Hairdressing
- Secretarial (in English-speaking countries).

If you own your own property in this country, letting it out might help to fund your time abroad until you find work.

Working abroad can be seen as an opportunity to gain valuable work and life experience; as a way of positively using the time you are unemployed; or as a more serious alternative to the lack of opportunities in this country. But it does need careful planning beforehand and a lot of thought needs to be put into the pros and cons. There are lots of good books now available which you should be able to find at your local reference library, such as the many publications by Vacation Work like *Work Your Way Round the World*; *Summer Jobs Abroad*; *Working in Ski Resorts*. There are also more general publications like *How to Get a Job Abroad* by Roger Jones and the fortnightly publication *Overseas Jobs Express*. If your library doesn't have anything, ask them to either buy suggested books or order copies from other libraries.

Overseas Jobs Express
PO Box 22
Brighton BN1 6HX
Tel. 0273 440220
A fortnightly publication.

▪ VOLUNTARY SERVICE OVERSEAS (VSO)

Solicitors may be two a penny at the moment in Britain, but in the Pacific they are crying out for legal advisers. Jobs in the building trade might be in decline where you live, but in Kenya they want those skills.

If you want to make use of your skills and experience, and are over 20, then VSO might be for you. Jobs can be anywhere in developing countries, and although you can state a preference, the more flexible you are the more quickly you will get a placing. This isn't a scheme just for single students; couples are also welcome, particularly if both have skills to offer (although they no longer recruit people with children).

Selection is not guaranteed. After assessing your application, candidates are invited to interviews held in London, Manchester or Glasgow (expenses paid). If you are successful, you will be contacted to discuss suitable postings. Your air fares are paid for, you will receive a salary at the local rate of pay, and you will receive three grants: one to help you prepare for departure, one mid-way through your placement, and one on your return home. Placements are all for two-year periods. Their own survey shows that 90 per cent of people find jobs within six months of their return.

So if working abroad appeals, this might be one opportunity worth considering.

VSO
317 Putney Bridge Road
London SW15 2PN
Tel. 081 780 2266

▪ CREATE A JOB

The normal way people go about finding employment is to scan around to find a job description that fits their own interests, experience, skills and qualifications. You might like to think about turning this around. Identify your particular strengths and build a job description around it. Identify the field you would most like to work in and contact relevant businesses. Market what you have to offer; point out the benefits to their organization; give them some very sound reasons why they should consider the opportunity you are offering them. For example, you might like to contact your local Adult Education College to discuss running a course for them which draws on the vast amount of expertise you might have. Or you might have excellent childcare skills which you could use to create and run a crèche for a local business.

This approach requires a lot of thought and market research to make sure that the demand for your created job is there, but it might be a more fruitful way forward than waiting to find a suitable job to be advertised and then have to compete with two hundred other applicants.

▪ SETTING UP A JOBCLUB

Jobclubs are places where you can go if you are long-term unemployed and which provide the necessary support to help you find work. They supply free of charge all the resources you might need, including telephones, stationery, typewriters, photocopier, directories, newspapers, stamps etc. There's possibly one in your area. If not, you might like to know that funding to set up and run a Jobclub is allocated on a competitive tendering basis ie you can put in a proposal and bid to your Regional Employment Service to run one yourself with their help and advice. If you don't feel you have the skills yourself, you may have to 'buy' them in, and include the costs in the budget proposal you submit.

Even if there is a general one where you live, there may be the opportunity to set up another which targets a special group of people eg the homeless, people with a disability, people who need help with their literacy. If you can show there is a need, you might be in with a chance.

Contact: Your Regional Employment Service. Address from the Job Centre or in your local telephone directory.

▪ It All Helps

Without a job it may seem impossible to maintain your CV and keep your skills alive. And without a current CV, successfully applying for jobs becomes that much more difficult. Consider ways in which you can not only keep your CV 'live', but also develop it. Besides a CV, you might also like to consider developing a Skills Portfolio. This is a list of skills which you have acquired and developed through experience, but not necessarily through employment. For example, someone who has been at home bringing up children could put down time management and budgeting on their list. Think about the many different areas of your life and spend some time identifying marketable skills, and if you know what sort of jobs you will be applying for, then you should obviously gear a description of your skills towards that specific goal by including only those that are relevant.

With this in mind, any work you do can be of use. Even if you consider yourself a manager, spending time doing manual work becomes not a demeaning prospect, but the opportunity to give you hands-on experience of shop-floor practice and an appreciation of what it's like to be on the receiving end of either good or bad management practice. Even Harrods' chairman, Mohamed Al Fayed, sees the benefit of this and regularly spends time working on the shop floor.

Seen in this context any work, paid or unpaid, also becomes valuable and another useful tool to help you ultimately find the job you want. Along these lines you might also consider setting up your own work experience programme by contacting businesses direct and explaining that you would like to do work experience with them for a number of weeks, or to work-shadow someone. The additional benefit of this is that it will not affect your benefits (although you have to tell them what you are doing when you sign on) *and* it puts you in the right place to hear about vacancies as they arise. It's also not uncommon for work experience placements to turn into actual jobs at the end of the placement period. At the very least, if you have made a good impression, they will think of you when something does come up at a later date.

Any paid or unpaid work can provide you with an opportunity to capitalize on the experience. I'm not suggesting for one moment that anyone should be made to take the nearest job to hand, but I do think it is worthwhile considering how you can use available job opportunities to help to:

- Fund you until you can do what you really have your sights set on, just as 'resting' actors do.
- Give you a chance to experience different sorts of work which you wouldn't otherwise.
- Develop your skills portfolio.
- Experience life in other countries.
- Gain a different perspective on life.
- Identify different job opportunities.
- Work towards your real goal on a practical and personal level.

Time spent out of regular paid employment can still provide you with many opportunities to spend the time positively, helping you reach the place where you really want to be. While we stay blinkered with sights set only on hunting out the nine to five job which may or may not exist, we cut ourselves off from, literally, a whole world of experiences, one of which might surprisingly lead you indirectly to your own personal Holy Grail.

In being out of work, most people look for a job which is similar to their last one. If you were a bank worker, you will probably be looking for a job in another bank. If you were a machine setter in a factory, you too will probably be looking for another machine setting vacancy. This is understandable. We have skills and experience which we want to put to use, and although it is unsettling to move to a different place of work, we at least feel comfortable with the familiarity and demands of the job. If you are young, you may simply be floundering as you try to find any job to provide you with a first foot-hold in the world of employment.

There is a wise saying which goes: 'If you want to be happy, find something you love doing so much that you would do it for free — then do it so well that people will pay you to do it for them' (*First Find Your Hilltop* by Roy Calvert et al). This can be applied to finding employment just as much as running your own business to which it refers, and it is a useful starting point in identifying how best to move forward.

'But I enjoyed my job in the bank/bakery/broom factory,' you might cry. Perhaps so, but it may have been just as much to do with enjoying the company of your work colleagues, the convenience of the job and how it fitted into your lifestyle or the pay you received, as much as it was to do with enjoying the work per se. Whatever job it was, whatever skills you were using, if you haven't been successful in finding another then it may be time to look at broadening your skills base and thinking of moving on, perhaps in a slightly different direction.

Having said that, going on a training course is no guarantee of a job at the end of it. Although you might have the essential qualification, you might find there are other blocks put in your way, such as lack of experience or age. This is where that quotation becomes so important. If you are going to look for a new skill to acquire, make sure it is something that you are wholeheartedly wanting to do. Make sure that when you have finished the course it will give you skills which you will want to use, for free if need be, not because you 'have to' to keep them up to date, but because you have a *need to* out of a sense of personal fulfilment and simply because using your new-found skills gives you such enjoyment — regardless of whether someone pays you or not. You feel that you want to go on learning about this new area you have entered, developing different ways of applying your skills, surprising people with your offers to put them into practice for free. It's like artists who create pictures because they feel a deep need to express themselves in that way, regardless of whether anyone buys their work; not having someone buy their latest piece never stopped any of those great artists in the past from picking up their brushes.

Signing onto just any training course may prove to be a futile exercise. Too many people are painfully aware that a qualification is no golden guarantee of a job. But you are in an excellent position of having the time to think carefully about what new skills you would like to add to your collection. You also have the time to investigate lots of different avenues; time which you probably never had while you were in employment, and which might not be there tomorrow. To take advantage, again think in terms of only having, say, three or six months without work at your disposal. How can you make the most of this time? What skills would you like to acquire by the time it is up? What can you do now before the time disappears?

Obviously one tends to think of training for new skills in a solely job-focused light. But regardless of whether you immediately find work, acquiring and using new skills can also give you:

• a sense of accomplishment

• satisfaction

• enjoyment

• a new direction

- a new focus

- renewed sense of self-esteem

- new contacts.

In fact, it can provide you with many of the elements which a job of work does — without the aggravation of a boss telling you what to do or having to take part in the commuter's nine-to-five nightmare routine.

So let's have a look at some different reasons for taking up a course or acquiring new skills, *besides* as an aide to employment (although all have the potential to lead into employment in one way or another — if you can spot how).

▪ NEW LIFESTYLE, NEW SKILLS

Inevitably one's lifestyle changes when you're unemployed. The old way becomes difficult or even impossible to keep up without the necessary income to support it. So much of what we do and focus on tends to depend upon money or material things. Even if it is only for a limited length of time, being without work enables you to sit back and reflect on your current lifestyle and how it could be changed to accommodate the new situation. Of course it may not be forever, but even so, it would be comforting to know that if unemployment were to strike again you would have the necessary skills to support you.

In reassessing, you may already have decided that this is the chance to make some very radical changes, like emigrating or becoming self-employed or relocating to another part of the country. These changes also provide opportunities to learn and develop, and it might even be necessary to acquire new skills to facilitate the change you want.

Many new skills could help you and your family become more self-sufficient (see Chapter 12). Learning how to take part in child care and household activities might be necessary. Budgeting, financial planning and handling debt might require specific new skills. Learning how to entertain yourself, family and friends at little or no cost may be necessary. So too might be learning how to make the best, constructive use of your time, which is also a skill in itself. And if you are seeing unemployment as the opportunity you have perhaps unconsciously been looking for to re-evaluate your life's overall direction, this too might require some new skills.

· FOR SAVING MONEY

There seems to be a curious anomaly which I realized when I started work: it's incredibly expensive to do it! Fares, lunches, clothes and their upkeep, socializing. It all adds up to a phenomenal amount, and more than once I had the distinct impression that I was going to work to earn the money to pay for the cost of going to work. Crazy. Luckily, being without a job enables you to eliminate those work costs straight away.

Besides immediate savings there are also lots of other ways in which even more money can be saved by learning to do a lot of things for yourself. When you are holding a job down there is precious little time to devote to many of life's household and other chores. We tend to pay someone to do it for us (which means we have to continue working to earn the money to pay them). If you previously paid an accountant to fill in your tax return, now you have the chance to learn how to do it yourself. The same with mending the car, baking bread, making wine, collecting herbs, plumbing, household repairs, rug making, etc. Spend some time listing all the different things you spend your money on and how it could be saved if you had the skills to do the job yourself. The limit only depends on how ambitious you want to be. Learning how to make jam might be your limit, or you might want to learn electronics so that you can assemble solar panels to cut down on heating and lighting overheads. Even building your own home could end up on your list.

• To Improve Your Quality of Life

If you have been unemployed for some time, lack of money can make it seem that the quality of your life has really taken a nose-dive. Now you have the chance to think about this issue for a while. What does 'quality of life' mean to you? Does it revolve around wanting more non-essential (or even essential) things? Does it mean the type of food eaten (see chapters 12 and 14)? Does it mean good health (see Chapter 14)? Does it mean quality leisure time (see Chapter 11)? It probably means a mix of lots of different things for different people.

Consider your quality of life and how you could improve it. It might be that you feel that if only you could afford a better Christmas, life throughout the year would seem better. You might feel that if only you didn't have to live on baked beans any more, your life would improve one hundred per cent. Whatever it is you can identify, take it on board and see how you could address the issue. You may feel that you lack the skills 'to do anything about it'. If so, add the little word 'yet' onto the end of that statement. It has the magical effect of giving you the chance to move forward. That dreary Christmas could be transformed by planning ahead and learning how to make quality gifts, decorations and cards, perhaps from recycled materials to keep the cost down even more; learn how to make your own wines and beers from the plants which nature gives us for free; plan a special whirl of party games and activities for the day; build a Christmas day menu around food which you can (in the main) grow yourself. And the unappetizing baked beans could be jettisoned in favour of some delicious, cheap and nutritious feasts, the result of some newly acquired cooking skills.

Take each issue in your life in turn and see it not as a block, but as a chance to learn new skills to transform your life for the better.

• Long-Term Goals

Have your vision of how you see your life in the future, and hold onto it. You might want to be the most successful business person ever, but right now you seem to have a fist full of qualifications and experience, or a youthful keenness which no one seems to want. But if you hold onto your vision of how you see yourself in the future, you might realize that there are lots of skills which you can learn now to help you take another step towards it. My nephew joined a business skills course, and it is now proving its worth in helping him towards self-employment. It isn't possible for him to take the giant step of running his own business all in one go, but he is taking smaller, bite-sized steps to edge his way forward more slowly, but still just as surely.

Think about what your long-term goals are and whether you too can take some smaller steps towards it. Few jobs demand the use of only the one skill, so think about more peripheral activities which might also help. For example, learn about interpersonal skills if reaching your goal will involve you working as part of a team; learn book-keeping if you want to work in a shop. Once you start making a move towards your goal, you will be surprised at how you will be helped along the way, probably from the most unexpected sources. I landed my first work as a writer through meeting someone on a business course (which had nothing directly to do with writing at all). In chatting to her and telling her what I was interested in she later sent me a small advertisement she had spotted in her local paper and which she encouraged me to apply for. The step I had taken in moving forwards helped not only in teaching me the business skills I needed, but it also indirectly gave me a helping hand from a very unexpected source indeed.

▪ FOR YOURSELF

I am sure the majority of us have little pockets of day-dreams sitting patiently, waiting for their time to come. 'I always wanted to have a go at . . .' might be how one of your day-dreams voices itself. Well, what the hell. Now you have the time available, think about having a go at all those things you always fancied having a dabble at, just for the sheer thrill and enjoyment of what it gives you, whether it's throwing a pot on a potter's wheel, or flinging pizza dough into the air and catching it.

Other courses might be just for 'you' in a different way, such as assertiveness training, or any course that you feel would boost your self-esteem. Skills aren't always job-related, but learning skills to improve your sense of self are just as valid and life enhancing as learning business, office or manufacturing skills and they will certainly translate into usefulness at interview.

So spend some time thinking about not only what you would like to have a go at, but also of other skills to learn which will be of direct benefit to you in a more personal way (see also Chapter 5).

▪ Where to Train

Government-sponsored Training

Find out what government-sponsored training courses are available where you live through your local Job Centre. The advantage of going on one of these, if you are eligible, is that:

- they are free
- your benefits are not affected
- you may receive an additional training allowance
- you may get your travel expenses refunded, in full or in part
- you will not have to go to 'sign on' while you're on the course.

People up to 18 (older if you have special needs) can also find out what Youth Training courses are available through their local Careers Service.

Private Colleges

If you have only recently lost your job you may not yet be eligible to join a government-sponsored course. However, if you have the funds available, there are many private colleges which offer training courses throughout the year, such as West Dean College which is specifically craft-based. Go to your local reference library or Careers Office, scan the classified advertisements in relevant magazines or ask people working in the field you're interested in if they can direct you to suitable colleges and courses.

West Dean College
West Dean
Chichester
West Sussex PO18 0Q2
Tel. 024363 301

Although it is unlikely you will be eligible for a grant for these types of courses, you might be able to find help through a charitable body or bursary scheme which the college or course organizers operate. Check out things like the government's Career Development Loan scheme which may lend you the money for fees — but it is repayable. Ask at your local Job Centre for details.

Adult Education Colleges

Courses which are offered through these local colleges are fantastic value for money. Courses may or may not lead to a qualification. Many classes are run simply for the pure enjoyment of those who want to learn how to re-upholster, make cabinets, cook special meals or otherwise investigate their creative talents.

With special rates for people who are unemployed, this could be an excellent way in which to acquire those practical (and other) skills you have identified.

Your local library should have copies of current prospectuses for local colleges. And if you cannot find the course you want, but can prove there is a demand, you can always approach the college with the suggestion that they supply the course you need. Check it out.

Skill-Share Scheme

There is probably another unemployed person in your locality right now who could really make use of the skills you already possess. Similarly, there is probably someone else who already has the cabinet-making skills you would like to acquire. Skill-share/swap schemes make use of this vast pool of under-used expertise.

You might be surprised to find that such a scheme already exists in your area. Find out by contacting your local Citizens Advice Bureau, library or unemployed workers' centre. If there isn't one running, why not start one? You might be able to start it off on a very informal footing, by mentioning it to a few people who you already know. Skills, whether they are 'taught' to someone eg how to service a car, or whether they are offered by the person to actually do the job, are all offered free. There is no value placed on whatever skill is transferred or work done. People receive their 'payment' when they next need something doing themselves, or want to be shown how to do it by someone.

Although the larger the pool of people involved the better, you may find it starts to generate running costs. Some could be offset by charging a small annual fee to members but this may still not be enough to cover it all. You could apply for help from:

- your local church
- Adult Education College
- Unemployment 'drop-in' centre
- Local Council through the Urban Aid scheme, or others
- any other local organizations or charities
- local businesses
- national charities
- anyone or anywhere which could offer non-cash contributions.

Training Through Other Agencies

There may be a number of voluntary or church organizations in your area which also offer training courses. For example, where

CAREERS

I live the local church offers upholstery, woodworking and sewing classes which are open for unemployed people to join. Have a look around at what different organizations are offering in your own locality. Go and visit them to find out. If they don't have anything on offer, ask if they know of places which do and follow up the leads they give you. Your local library or community notice board may also carry details and so might your local paper. If, through your research, you unearth a wealth of available training opportunities which have previously remained hidden, think about how you could use that knowledge — perhaps by producing a brochure which lists what's on. On the other hand, if you find there isn't anything available at all, read on to Chapter 10.

Being unemployed brings with it many difficulties, some of which can't be overcome without the job to bring in a more significant income. While you endeavour to find that work, or until your vision for your future becomes manifest, there is a wonderful opportunity to turn the time available to you (which might turn out to be very limited) into a period in your life which not only gives you something in return but which also enriches you. Endeavouring to learn new skills will bring about the sense that you are in fact moving forward. And if the courses aren't there for you, see that as an opportunity, too. If you can prove the need, funds may be available to run the course, either through your local Adult Education College, Training and Enterprise Council, other local run initiative, or perhaps through a local church. As they say, where there's a will, there's a way.

5 ▪ *Flex Those Mental Muscles*

The last chapter talked about the many advantages of, and reasons for, acquiring new skills. But not everyone feels they have an aptitude or even interest in the more practical aspects of life. My father would be someone who would fit into that category, where changing a light bulb would be a major feat. However, his time without work since being retired has been devoted to reading, and study in the informal sense.

Much is written about the need to exercise the body and the benefits from doing so. Less is written about the need to exercise the mind, even though body and mind are so closely interconnected. Training for top sports people concentrates not just on the physical, but also on the mental aspects of performing well. Similarly, although we're not aiming to be a top athlete we generally look after our bodies and attend to them when they feel below par; but our minds tend to be overlooked, and not exercised at all well. A diet of worry about being unemployed, supplemented with mind-dulling, easy-viewing television is not particularly nourishing.

Think of the mind as a sort of muscle. Flex it regularly, put it through its paces, keep it on a healthy diet, and like your physical body it too will respond in kind. Study may be the opportunity which presents itself to you now while you're unemployed and since it is by no means the sole preserve of the young, this could be the option for you whether you're 25 or 55.

▪ WHY STUDY?

As with acquiring new skills, there are many reasons for studying. The most obvious one to spring to your mind right now will probably be in order to gain qualifications and improve your chances of getting a job. Study for this reason needs serious consideration. If you are young and not long out of education, gaining a higher qualification in a subject will help. Employers are obviously looking for the best qualified to fill a vacancy and with a paper qualification being one measure of suitability for a job, it will help you stay in with a chance during the weeding out process. However, for older job candidates who have taken time out to gain a degree, apparently there is no indication that just having a degree per se improves your chance of getting a job (*The Mature Student's Handbook*; Margaret Korving). The situation is different if the qualification relates to a particular job. So if you know where you are heading and what your ultimate goal is, taking a course of study may be of help if it is specific to that goal. For example, having a degree in Social Science may not be of much help if you have your heart set on moving into marketing; having an MBA might.

If you are thinking of study in a solely work-related light, it would be wise to consider carefully whether it will ultimately be of real use to you. If in doubt, get as much advice as you can from people who are already working in your chosen field, such as employers, employees, trade unions, professional associations, and so on. It might also be helpful to discuss your plans with a tutor on the course you have in mind. They should have a good knowledge, not only about what occupations their students go into, but also what employers are looking for in your chosen field.

Your own experience may guide you as to what might be helpful to study. If the jobs you are wanting to apply for all ask for a minimum qualification which you don't have, then it is quite obvious what you should do. For example, although someone may have a number of years' experience as a nursery assistant they may find themselves having no success in their job applications because most employers now only want people who have the NNEB qualification. If you have lots of experience in business, but are having no success with job applications, or in the speculative approaches to potential employers, a relevant higher qualification may help.

Studying is not only of use to people who have already worked in their chosen field, and who are simply looking to improve their chances of impressing the person who is short-listing applications; it may also be of use to those who have embarked on reassessing their career aims. For those who have decided that now is the time to make a change of direction in their career, studying might be the way to help that change become manifest. As before, it is vital that you take as much professional advice as you can to ensure that you choose the most appropriate course of study, and that it really will provide you with the best leverage into eventual employment.

But although employment will obviously be your major concern, we are forgetting that studying just for pure enjoyment's sake is also valid enough reason to do it. Finding a course of study which really interests you, genuinely fires your curiosity, and rouses you from your mental doze and slumbers can bring you lots of additional benefits, aside from simply learning something new:

- regular attendance at classes can help provide you with a sense of purpose.
- studying can often help to open up other new avenues of enquiry.
- it is an opportunity to meet other people with similar interests.
- flexing those mental muscles has the knock-on effect of enlivening the rest of you.
- feeling stronger mentally can help you feel better about being able to cope with sorting out other problems in your life.
- it can help to start rebuilding your confidence if it has become somewhat depleted.
- although a short course in studying local history won't be of direct relevance to applying for a job as an engineer, including it on your CV will help to keep it live, and give

an indication to the employer of just how interesting a person you are (I feel sure that putting down my basic qualification in Wines and Spirits under 'Interests and hobbies' on applications forms, helped my applications along in the past!). Think about it. Employers who are always mindful of costs wouldn't waste space on application forms to include the hobbies and interests question if there wasn't good reason.

- it could turn into a more serious form of study.
- it may give you some ideas for a career change.
- it may give you an idea for starting your own business.
- meeting more people increases your chances of casually hearing about job vacancies as they arise, and before they are advertised.
- doing something you enjoy will inevitably cheer you up and help to lift those unemployment blues.

Besides taking part in formal courses, there are other ways in which you can study. In considering your present situation, you may be coming to some profound realizations about how you would ideally like to live your life from now on, or how you would like to insure against falling foul of the system in the future. These realizations may call for dramatic changes. If the new direction is appropriate for you and will help you along the path to true fulfilment and understanding of your life's real aim, the path will seem much easier for you. For example, when I was unemployed I wasn't too sure initially about where I was going in life although I did know that I wanted to work for myself. I knew nothing about how to go about it, but finding a suitable course was so easy that it seemed to almost fall into my lap. I knew then that I was at least heading in the right direction.

Similarly you might be coming to some decisions which require you to enter previously uncharted territory. Knowledge will help you navigate your way through. It is always available to you, and in many different guises — not necessarily in the form of classes. You can embark on your own private study course which you can plan out and develop yourself. Unlike a lot of courses where you are expected to sit through all of it when you might only be interested in a quarter of its contents, you can produce a study plan which is tailor-made to fit your own interests, needs and aims. And it won't cost you anything!

Once you know what knowledge you need to acquire, you can launch yourself into your own private research:

- Libraries. Even if you only have access to a small local branch, they can always acquire books for you on request, either by buying them in or by borrowing them from another library. It may take some time, but most books can always be located, even if they have to come from the British Library. And the bliss of libraries is that they are free — and centrally heated!
- People. For example, if you have decided that you want to adopt a totally alternative lifestyle, talk to sympathetic friends and acquaintances about your ideas. Ask them for any useful information or suggestions they might have. Do they know of anyone who is doing what you want to do? Can they suggest any good books on the subject? It's a case of 'Ask and it shall be given.'
- Non-fiction books may provide you with a useful list of relevant organizations. Write to them. The book may also leave you with unanswered questions. If so, write to the author, c/o the publisher whose address is printed at the front of the book.
- Charities, research bodies and other professional or even voluntary organizations might be able to provide you with the information you want in order to help you along with your studies.

Some people feel motivated enough to study alone. However, others work best by being part of a group. This isn't a problem if you're on a formal study course, but if you are directing your own study you might find that you would like to talk to others who are interested in the same topic, to help each other out and exchange ideas. If so, you could consider forming a study group. It would be easy enough to start: advertise in your local newsagent's window, on local community notice boards or through other groups which you may be a member of, such as a church, and then find somewhere to meet. You may be happy to take it in turns to have the meeting at each other's houses, but if not see if a local college, community centre, church or library would offer you the space for free, or in exchange for lending a helping hand for an hour or so. Chapter 10 goes into setting up a group in more detail.

▪ WHAT'S AVAILABLE

There is a vast range of study courses on offer, ranging from purely academic to 'just for fun'.

GCSE and A Levels

These courses are provided through local adult education colleges and also some colleges of further education. Call in for their current prospectuses or consult these at your local library. If you are not close to any local facilities, a correspondence course might be more suitable but fees will be involved. The National Extension College, which is perhaps the best known correspondence college, offers a discount if you are unemployed and also provides useful advice on grants and loans for which you may be eligible to apply. They currently offer over 125 different courses. For a list of courses offered by accredited correspondence colleges, contact the Council for the Accreditation of Correspondence Colleges.

Degree Courses

If you didn't go to college or university after leaving school, now might be a good time to consider catching up on those missed opportunities. Doing a degree may be your way of chasing your dream, regardless of age. Degree courses are not just for 18 year olds and colleges and universities welcome mature students. 'Mature' means anyone who is 25 at the start of the intended course.

The National Extension College
18 Brooklands Avenue
Cambridge CB2 2HN
Tel. 0223 316644

The Council for the Accreditation of
Correspondence Colleges
27 Marylebone Road
London NW1 5JS
Tel. 071 935 5391

Although A levels are a prerequisite if you are applying to do a degree straight from school, the rules are different for mature students. Quite rightly they see that a lot of valuable learning will have been acquired which can be brought to the course. If you have acquired other qualifications along the way which can demonstrate your level of ability they will take this into account, such as Open University credits. They will also look favourably if you have attended a Return to Study or similar course at an Adult Education College. If you have no qualifications to show, they will still accept your application and will explain to you what they require from you to demonstrate that the course would be suitable for you. They may offer an assessment under an Assessment of Prior Experiential Learning scheme; invite you to take an entrance exam; invite you to prepare a portfolio to demonstrate your abilities through reference to the type of work you have done, the responsibilities you have assumed and any other relevant information — rather like an extended CV.

If you have not had a grant before for higher education, and will have lived in this country for three years prior to the start of the course, you should be eligible for a grant. The amount varies from year to year and according to your personal circumstances and is now complicated by the student loan scheme. To see if you are eligible, go to the education department at your local town hall and ask for information about applying for grants. Your local library should also have relevant information. Otherwise, contact the Department for Education for their free booklet, *Student Grants and Loans*.

Department for Education
Sanctuary Buildings
Great Smith Street
London SW1P 3BT
Tel. 071 925 5000

Open University

Most people have heard of the Open University. By studying at home, with the help from regular meetings with a tutor and occasional residentials, you build up to a degree through completing a number of units of study. Your study is flexible in so far that you could begin studying for your degree now and take ten years to complete it, if so desired. However, the disadvantage with studying through this organization is that fees are involved, so while you may have the time to dedicate, you may not necessarily have the funds available to finance it while being unemployed. Having said this, they do offer payment by instalment and there may be financial awards available through them towards the cost of the course. They also offer non-degree courses for personal and leisure interests, health and social welfare, and others.

Correspondence Courses

Besides courses which lead to either GCSEs or A levels, there are lots of other correspondence courses available. The

National Extension College has already been mentioned, and they too offer a whole range of different courses besides the ones mentioned, from personal development through to business and degree courses.

Central Enquiry Service
The Open University
PO Box 200
Milton Keynes MK7 6YZ
Tel. 0908 653231

If you are wanting to help yourself reach the new goal you have identified for yourself, but have drawn a blank in terms of finding a suitable 'statutory' course to attend, a correspondence course may offer what you want. Again, your library may be your best initial port of call for information. If you are looking for something quite specific, you could contact the relevant professional body and again your librarian should help you find their address. Relevant magazines also often advertise courses which would appeal to their readership. For example, if you are interested in learning about astrology and have failed to find a local course, *Prediction* magazine carries advertisements for a range of correspondence courses.

If you have decided that a correspondence course is just what you are looking for, it is much better if you can find someone who can recommend a suitable one. You don't want to hand over your money in good faith only to find that the course of study is not suitable. If you have any doubts, check with the relevant professional body, or with the Council for the Accreditation of Correspondence Colleges, address page 57. Regard with suspicion those who show scant regard for your concerns, and always make sure you read the small print before making any financial commitment.

Understandably your focus right now is probably on simply getting a job and on ways to improve the success rate of job applications. Studying to improve your qualifications may help, but embarking on a course of study can also help in more subtle ways. What you might initially think of as a detour into study and away from your job-seeking objective, may prove to bring you more directly to the point you were bound for — perhaps without you even knowing what that point was. With any study, whether for skills or knowledge or interest, follow your heart and the benefits will soon be felt.

For those with a sagging waistline and whose toes haven't been seen from the vertical since long time past, you'll be pleased to know that self-development doesn't refer to body-building work outs. Instead, self-development means starting to learn about what constitutes your real self, your inner self, your true self and about how to bring that into being. The majority of us tend to live lives driven by what is called our ego or outer needs, like when we believe we will be happier with a bigger, better car, or when our job status gives us our sense of worth. These are all outer 'dressings'. Gradually there comes a time, sooner or later, when these outer trappings are seen as somehow insufficient for our needs; the initial glow they gave us fades; we are left feeling empty, dissatisfied, unfulfilled. Some seek to alleviate this by buying an even bigger car or finding another position with even more status, only to find they eventually reach the same point again. The spiral continues. Others slowly come to act on that sense of dissatisfaction and realize that if the first car didn't do the trick and bring lasting happiness, then it is unlikely a second one would either.

Being unemployed can be seen as a useful short-cut to reaching that point of realization quickly; but the majority only see unemployment in terms of unfairness and 'Why me?' Rage at feeling the injustice of having our outer wants for material comforts curbed is understandable; it is also difficult to cope with. It brings scant comfort or credibility if someone says, 'Well, you wouldn't be satisfied with those things anyway,' when you are desperately trying to pay the gas bill or find enough money for a bus fare. Those problems are only too real and are not to be made light of, but although they may not disappear without the help of paid employment, the impact those difficulties have on our sense of worth and inner happiness *can* be changed.

People who are busy holding down jobs are constantly distracted from themselves. Their lives are often so demanding that the only way in which they can make them more tolerable is to spend more and more money on buying things in an attempt to bring some sense of comfort into their lives. Take away those comforts and they realize just how uncomfortable their lives really are. Even with material luxuries, many eventually begin to feel the same sense of discomfort and unease (normally during the mid-life crisis). And so you could look on people in employment with a certain sense of pity. They are held captive by their more comfortable lifestyle, whereas you have been provided with a set of circumstances which could bring about a great awakening within you (although it may seem more like a rude awakening right now). As I mentioned before, I believe none of us, no matter what hand we are dealt by life, are given anything more than we can cope with. Soft living gives us few clues to what life is really about. Hard living, and it can be incredibly hard being unhappily unemployed, always teaches more. So if you're feeling that things are particularly difficult right now, understand that you must be a pretty tough person to be given these things to deal with. You are stronger than you perhaps yet know. Difficult tasks are only given to those most able to carry them out. In that respect you are streaks ahead of the office workers sitting pretty in their easy chairs.

But in being thrust into these circumstances, you may well wonder just what it is you are waking up to. The answer has to be, 'Yourself'. You may be in a position where the main resource — money — has all but disappeared. Many other physical resources may also have disappeared from your life, including friends, your own transport, your overdraft facility, credit cards. But the one incredibly powerful resource which you do have is your true self. No one can take that away, and it is the one thing that is more powerful and potent than any of those outer trappings. It is so powerful that you may even come to the certainty that it can affect your outer reality in whatever way you choose. All this time it has been waiting quietly in the wings, watching while your other selves have taken centre stage. The circumstances are now right for you to invite your true self to come forward and let itself be known, while your other outer selves have fallen away, sulking in the side-lights because you haven't any more new toys with which to keep them amused. Bringing your true self forward is what self-development is all about. Who knows, it may be one of the reasons why you are in the situation you are in now. Circumstances may have conspired to give you the breathing space in which you can meet your real self. Being unemployed may have been the only way in which your real inner needs could be brought to your attention. In the normal hum-drum of life it is only too easy to ignore that small voice in the wings.

Self development is your new insurance policy. In discovering your own power, your sense of self will no longer be at the mercy of others' whims. You will not feel destroyed if there is a next time when someone says, 'Sorry, but there's no more work for you here.'

But what does 'getting to know yourself' actually mean?

In a way we are like grown-up children, but children none the less. We tend to be driven by wants, 'I want this,' 'I want that,' although we may dress up the language to sound rather more sophisticated. We ask people 'What do you do?' when we first meet them, and then ask them 'What are you doing at the weekend?' when we know them a bit better. We tend to operate for the majority of the time on these superficial and 'doing' levels which provides few opportunities to question at a deeper level. Getting to know your self better goes beyond this superficiality. It will help you understand *why* you think you need certain things. Fully understanding your motivation helps you to make appropriate choices more easily.

Going within will help you to understand more fully your strengths — and your weaknesses. Facing up to our vulner-abilities can seem like a frightening thing to do, but it allows us to be braver in situations where we might feel threatened, intimidated or unsure of ourselves. Accepting those weaknesses allows us to define them more clearly, see them better, and start to work out how best to work with them. Finding out what our strengths are allows us to see the good material we can work with straight away. Getting to know these aspects of ourselves may help us to see more clearly not only which direction we should be moving in but can also help us to appreciate our feelings of self-worth. We may not have a job, but it doesn't stop us from cherishing our strengths and nurturing our weaknesses.

Inevitably during the process of starting to become more familiar with your true self, you will come across blockages; inner blockages which stop you from making any progress. For example, you may have an aversion to acknowledging and accepting a certain unpleasant aspect of your character, or you may become aware that you avoid specific difficult situations or topics of conversation; you may begin to notice that you experience difficulties in handling some types of emotions either within yourself or in others. We all have such blockages; remnants from the process of growing up which now act as defences to protect our vulnerabilities. Lack of assertiveness and over-aggressiveness are two common ways in which we seek to maintain those defences. Neither is effective and only serve to keep us in emotional strait-jackets, preventing us from moving forward emotionally.

Blockages are closely linked with our belief systems ie those rules which we have learned and which may have been valid in the past but which have now outworn their usefulness. Inappropriate belief systems can block our necessary growth. For example, believing that 'Girls don't do dirty jobs' or that 'Men can't be secretaries' could be holding you back from developing an aspect of yourself which has been dying to come out. Believing that 'I just couldn't apply for/do that job' which may carry responsibilities and offer to put you in the limelight could be the sort of belief which is halting your progress. Believing you can't do something because it seems out of character, or because no one of your age/experience/

background has done anything like that before is the sort of thought which holds you back from life and from fully investigating the whole range of your potential.

If your self has previously been defined by your job, it will be inevitable that in losing it your self-esteem will also seem to have been lost as well. If this is the case for you, there may be a small voice inside saying that feeling this way just can't be right. No job = no person? Surely not. That voice is correct, yet without a strong sense of self-esteem it may seem to you that until another job comes along to give you a feeling of justification in other people's eyes, then you almost don't count. This isn't true, and through developing your sense of self you will come to find that in fact your worth is immeasurable; that you are an incredibly valuable person, with or without a job. And in coming to realize this, your confidence will automatically start to increase; it will begin to show when you meet new situations, when you fill in application forms and when you attend interviews. And even if you receive another rejection, with a greater sense of self-worth and confidence you will more easily be able to bounce back, ready to try again.

Lack of confidence can really undermine people's performance in life, both in specific situations and in general. This may be one of your difficulties, leaving you with a vague sense of grinding along in a low gear when really you should be shooting off into the stars and beyond. Building up your confidence will help you do exactly that, and it doesn't depend on whether you have a job or not. It does depend on a willingness to start learning about yourself.

It can seem too risky to some people to embark on self-development if we sense it might challenge some of our dearly held personal beliefs. It does provide a huge challenge, but one which has big pay-offs if you meet it. In refusing to pick up the gauntlet, relationships may continue to prove difficult, self-esteem will constantly have to be shored up, vast new territories of unexplored potential within can simply go to waste amid the frustrations of trying to hold on to the status quo. We are dynamic beings, and we owe it to ourselves to grow and give ourselves the best chance possible.

The pay-offs from all this are well worth it:

- You will begin to feel better about yourself and your life.
- You will feel more able to cope with whatever life may come up with next.
- You will gain a better perspective on life. What may previously have seemed to be the end of the world, now becomes more of a challenge which you want to take on board.
- You will develop a much deeper sense of security; one which isn't based on having money in the bank or having someone to call 'boss', but which comes from within and which remains constant despite life's ups and downs.
- You can start to give yourself a chance.
- If you have felt demeaned by being unemployed, you will be able to start believing in yourself.
- Self-confidence, self-respect and self-esteem will be restored (or even discovered for the first time!).
- You will be able, at last, to identify what your *real* needs are and therefore stand a better chance of finding ways in which to have them met.

And on the more practical side:

- As you begin to develop you will start to come across more positively when you apply for jobs, and at interview.
- New avenues of discovery will start to open up.
- Discovering what your real needs are will be a guide to help you onto your true life path. This may mean a change of direction in your employment aims, a change of lifestyle, or other more radical changes.
- Once you have aligned yourself with your true life aims, you will find that support comes to you, perhaps from very unexpected sources.
- According to metaphysical law, the world around you

mirrors your world within. Improvements in your self should therefore be reflected in improvements in your life in general. Learning to value yourself (which can be difficult while you are unemployed when it seems like no one else values you) will lead to your outer self having its needs met.

It seems then that through self-development you have nothing to lose, and everything to gain. But how does one go about it?

There is a vast range of different ways in which to begin and reading this chapter has already given you a start, since it will have brought some issues to your attention. A useful way to consider the options is to divide them into four categories:

- Thinking, mental or intellectual

- Physical

- Emotional

- Psycho-spiritual.

▪ THINKING

Some people are more comfortable with starting to understand themselves through finding out all the facts first. What do the experts say? What do they recommend? If this is you, then starting off in this way will probably appeal most.

There are many books available which cover a whole range of topics under the self-development umbrella. Relevant books may be found under psychology, new age, metaphysics, religion, health, and careers. If you know where you want to start, then your task is obviously that much easier. For example, you might be aware that you are too passive and would like to be more assertive, in which case read something like *Assert Yourself* by Gael Windenfield. As you begin your studies you will start to find references to other texts to lead you on further.

If you don't know where to start, you could either go for a long browse around a bookshop or your library to see what catches your eye (it will inevitably be the right starting point for you), or you can read a more general text such as *In Search of Yourself* by Janet Dian, published by Expansions Publishing, 1991, and its follow-up, *Moving Forward*, or *Living Magically* by Gill Edwards, published by Piatkus, 1991. There are many different approaches to investigate, ranging from psycho-synthesis to metaphysics — complex-sounding names, but all have the simple aim of helping you to get to know yourself. Take the time to research the many ways forward. There is none which is better than another, only different ways to suit each of us as individuals.

Lectures may also appeal, so start to investigate what is on offer in your area. Your local library, community notice board or paper may advertise events. If nothing seems to take place of this sort you could arrange for guest speakers to come along and talk to a group of like-minded individuals. Your local church, college, Women's Institute or community worker might be able to help you organize it.

One distinct advantage of approaching self-development in this way is that it is cheap. It costs nothing to borrow books from libraries, and many lectures on these subjects are either free or offer concessionary rates.

• PHYSICAL

Our minds and bodies are inextricably interlinked. When we feel down, it is echoed in our low-key voice, lack of energy and poor posture. There are many physical therapies which can gain access to emotions and provide enormous relief by working through the body. For example, the Alexander Technique corrects postures and movements which may be sapping energy. Raising awareness about how you stand and move can bring insights into how you see yourself, how you come across to others, and reveal emotional blocks which may be affecting your body's own natural movements. There are books available on this and other therapies, some of which are particularly suitable to self-therapy such as Do-In, a therapy which helps relieve both physical and emotional difficulties through self-massage of specific pressure points on your body. Even learning about self-defence or taking gentle exercise such as T'ai Chi can help by increasing your feelings of self-confidence. Your local adult education college may offer classes in some of these and notice boards in health food shops may carry details of what's available locally. If not, there are lots of books available; contact your local library.

▪ EMOTIONAL

Thankfully, the public at large is becoming more educated about the role of psychotherapeutic practice. No longer is it seen as something which only mentally unstable or insane people need. Psychotherapy is a way in which you can perhaps best come to understand yourself and how you tick. Talking through your feelings with a therapist can help you safely to explore important issues which you wish to bring to each session. Through psychotherapy your awareness is raised to reveal issues which you may not have realized were proving to be so much a block in your life.

Therapy can be expensive, but there may be organizations in your area which offer either a free service or concessionary rates. Your local Citizens Advice Bureau may have local addresses, or contact: British Association for Counselling. A few enlightened GPs' surgeries may be able to put you in touch with someone through the NHS.

British Association for Counselling
1 Regent Place
Rugby
Warwicks CV21 2PJ
Tel. 0788 578328

If even the concessionary rates are too much, you may be able to afford group therapy sessions which are much cheaper. And if this still seems out of reach you could investigate co-counselling, where individuals help each other towards self-understanding. For further details send an SAE to Co-counselling International.

```
Co-counselling International
c/o Westerly
Prestwick Lane
Chiddingfold
Surrey GU8 4XW
Send an SAE with your enquiry.
```

▪ PSYCHO-SPIRITUAL

Ultimately, your true self already exists. It is already within, and any help from people 'outside' merely acts to enable you to gain access to it and bring it forth.

All psycho-spiritual techniques work by causing us to reflect on ourselves. Again there are many tools at your disposal, such as learning to read tarot cards, casting runes, shamanism, Zen, and so on. These might be areas you would like to investigate. Meditation may also be useful — and it doesn't cost anything.

In reality, you may find that you take a mix and match approach to your self-development, according to what you feel comfortable with and what your purse or wallet allows. But whichever approach you use, it will pay dividends. Self-development is perhaps the best tool at your disposal in helping you get back on your feet and start to make progress in your life and move forward. The insights you gain can help to clarify where you should be and what you should be doing with your life. And in the face of such rapid changes in life which can seem to overtake us, with a better insurance policy through self-development we will at least be able to weather what life throws at us and know how to turn circumstances to our best advantage. But for the present, it is only when we begin to change within that we will start to see a change without.

Think about whether this whole area offers any opportunities for you. Consider whether you could initiate or co-ordinate local interest. Perhaps other unemployed people are waiting for someone just like you to help start things going. Read Chapter 10 about ways in which to set up a group.

7 ▪ Creating Your Own Employment

What perverse creatures we are. When we are in work, the majority of us dream of holiday time when the nine to five can be left behind for a while, or of winning the pools so that work is no longer necessary, or even of retirement — the legitimate end to work. So why does being unemployed seem to create such misery? Apart from the obvious financial one, it is the growing sense of futility as yet another fruitless job enquiry fails, and the inevitable anger at having valuable skills, experience and enthusiasm which employers keep saying they don't want, thank you very much. It's a bit like setting up a market stall with all the items you are most proud of, only to have every single potential buyer who walks by, snub them — and you. But I don't need to tell you what it feels like.

The overwhelming feeling is one of powerlessness. You have the energy to put into the job search, but either the applications come to nothing (not even an interview to give you a chance to prove yourself), or there quite simply aren't the jobs available. I work for a charity, helping young people with moderate learning difficulties into employment and regularly make visits to local Job Centres. Although it may look like the boards are full of job vacancies, it doesn't take long to realize that each job is advertised about three or four times on different boards. Even the opportunity of finding suitable jobs to apply for is limited. Prospects seem very bleak.

So, what are the available options? You can continue your job search activities and remain one of the band of knights searching for the Holy Grail (they never did find it); you can diversify your search through training or alternative work options (see Chapter 3); or you can start to reclaim your own sense of power over the situation in which you find yourself. 'What, me? Power? Nah.' Well, if you say so, fine. But all that you have stopping yourself from moving forward is your sense of powerlessness, reinforced on a regular basis through a diet of rejection letters and unsuitable job ads. It is only a belief but unfortunately it may now have developed into something which feels more like an immovable object. Those feelings can be changed when you start to smell the sweet scent of opportunity blowing your way; when you can see that there might just be a possibility that there is another option, another way forward to lead out of unemployment. Creating your own employment could be that way. If employers don't want to give you a job, then why should you just let them make you believe that you have nothing to offer at all? You have. You also have power. So why not go ahead and create your own work for yourself (and possibly others, too), and start to exercise that sense of power which has taken a back seat for so long?

Being able to provide yourself with your own work relies less on having a rich uncle to back you than on knowing yourself well. The start of the book encouraged you to see your unemployment as an opportunity for reassessment: of your skills, talents or aptitudes, interests, experience and knowledge. Working for yourself provides the framework in which to create a tailor-made job for yourself which makes use of all your abilities — and you have many, whether it's a knack for story-telling, an avid interest in the music scene, or just being a dynamic personality. Your talents could provide you with the crock of gold you've been trying to find in the Jobs Vacant ads. As was mentioned in the last chapter, our happiness lies within. A job which provides the 'readies' will alleviate some of your angst, but just imagine what joy it would be to work at something which you would do even without pay, because you enjoy it so much. That's the way to real success and job satisfaction. Find your vision, your overall game plan, the way you see yourself living.

Perhaps you already have that vision without knowing it. If you have ever day-dreamed of how you would like to see yourself, that provides you with a clue as what you are about. For me, my day-dream was sitting at a table in front of open french windows which looked out onto a Mediterranean scene — and I was writing. It wasn't until I verbalized that 'day-dream' to someone that I started to make the move towards realizing it. Alright, so I'm not typing this in front of the Mediterranean scene — yet; but at least I am doing what I had only dreamed of before and I am in the process of making moves towards the idyllic setting.

And so you already have a lot of things going for you. You have an itinerary of all your saleable personal assets (ie what you can do), you have the need, which gives you the drive, and hopefully you have your vision. What a powerful combination! But if you don't have them yet, don't worry. Once you start to address yourself to the challenge and feel that yes, self-employment really could be just what you're looking for, then things will start to take shape. If it's for you, you will sense that somehow it just feels right, perhaps without being able to put it into words properly or even, at this stage, provide any facts to support the idea. Listen carefully to what your intuition says about it.

But it would be wrong of me to imply that working for yourself is for everyone without looking briefly at some of the pros and cons. Many new enterprises do go under at the rate of some 40 per cent in their first year, and 90 per cent within five years. Although these sound like very grim statistics, it is also true to say that 80 per cent of those who become self-employed, stayed self-employed. This means that even though people might start up a business which ultimately fails, they simply pick themselves up and start all over again. In America they say that you cannot call yourself a true entrepreneur until you have had three business failures. But even so, you want to aim for success, not failure, so do consider all aspects first:

Pros

- You have the chance to put your ideas, talents, enthusiasms etc. to good use — as your own employer, you will know how best to make use of what you have to offer.

- No more job application forms to fill in and no more rejection letters.
- You can feel more in control of your working life — you're the boss, and you decide what you should and shouldn't do.
- You can choose how to shape your business — you will no longer have to work at something you don't enjoy.
- You have a certain degree of control over who your customers are — although at first you might not be able to be so picky.
- Yes, your business might fail, but at least you are in a position to manage the risks yourself — unlike being employed by someone else (ask anyone who has been made redundant).
- You have a greater flexibility — no more commuting or nine-to-five routine.
- You are in a position to take advantage of opportunities as they present themselves to you.

And on the more community-minded level:

- Local businesses help local communities by keeping the money circulating within it (and hopefully bringing more money into it, too). In poor areas where there are fewer businesses around to generate a flow of cash, money leaches out of the area very quickly; in rich areas it tends to circulate lots of times before leaving, keeping the locality well nourished.

Cons

- You may have to work longer hours than if you were in employment.
- If the business goes under you may be left in debt — if you don't prepare for such contingencies.
- Raising enough money to start the business off may prove difficult (but not impossible).

- It can be very insecure, especially in the early days and if you are working as a sole trader.
- It can be bloody hard work!

Considering just how much hard work is involved in setting up and running a business, you may want to think about how you can find the much needed support to see you through. You could set up a support group, consisting of like-minded others who are also unemployed and considering self-employment as an option. In being in the same proverbial boat, you could share a lot of information and advice as well as give support and encouragement to each other. Basically it is the same concept which lies behind Chambers of Commerce or business clubs. Chapter 10 explains about setting up a group in more detail.

Even with this sort of networking and support behind you, you may still feel that it is too much for you to take on board on your own, or you know that quite simply you work best as a member of a team. Being a sole trader (ie you're the only 'boss-person') is not the only way in which to set up in business:

▪ PARTNERSHIPS

You may find that sharing the responsibilities with other people is more appealing. You could consider working with your husband, wife or live-in partner, a close friend, a colleague who you know shares the same interests, or you could advertise. Partnerships can consist of more than just two people.

Besides sharing responsibilities, there are other advantages to working in partnership:

- More money can be raised if more than one person is putting cash into the pot.
- Any losses are shared out equally between all partners, instead of having to be carried by one person alone.

- More groundwork can be covered — many hands etc.
- Each person can contribute a range of skills, which cuts down on the need to buy them in from outside.

But equally there can be drawbacks to working in partnerships:

- There may be disagreements over how the business is run.
- Resentments can easily build up if it seems that the workload is unevenly spread.
- Difficulties can arise if important decisions are taken without full consultation with the other partners.
- Partners may resent losses which are made by others.

These and other similar issues must be dealt with beforehand and it's advisable to have a formal agreement drawn up by a solicitor in order to protect everyone's interests. But even bearing in mind the potential difficulties in operating in partnership with others, it may be the most sensible, and desirable way forward. You could also consider forming a limited company which has the benefits of limiting how much each person is liable for, should the company go broke.

▪ CO-OPERATIVES

This is an excellent way of setting up in business. Basically, a co-op is a business just like any other, except that the running of it is controlled not by one boss but collectively by everyone who works in it: one member, one vote. Everyone has an equal say in what goes on. And unlike other employment, everyone has a share in the profits of the business. Co-ops can be set up to operate in any field, just like other businesses: manufacturing, providing a service, retailing etc. There are no special rules about what a co-op can or can't be set up to do.

Co-ops are becoming more popular by the year, perhaps because it is a realistic way in which people who wouldn't otherwise do so can set up their own local enterprise, supported with help from The Industrial Common Ownership Movement (ICOM) who offer advice about how to go about setting up and running a co-operative. You may have a local Co-operative Development Agency (CDA) which will do the same. Both agencies can also help you to arrange the financing of your venture and even help out with small sums to support initial costs or feasibility studies.

The Industrial Common Ownership Movement (ICOM)
Vassalli House
20 Central Road
Leeds LS1 6DE
Tel. 0532 461737/8

If you can get a small (or large) group interested, or you would simply like to know more, contact ICOM for further help or for the address of your local CDA.

▪ COMMUNITY BUSINESSES

As the name implies, community businesses are just like any other, but they are established to meet the needs of individual communities. Painting and decorating, craft centres, local events magazines, second-hand shops, cafes, drop-in centres for people who are unemployed, are all examples of community businesses; but basically anything goes, so long as it serves the needs of your community and it is a viable business.

A community is defined in its broadest sense: where you live, the common language you have, needs which you share in common, gender, and so on. If you feel that your community is depressed and could do with a particular service, or desperately needs a way in which to reduce unemployment, a community business could be the way forward. Why should communities have to 'buy in' expensive items which no one can really afford when it could produce its own at a cheaper rate, and get the community alive and working again?

Community businesses are similar to co-operatives in that they are run collectively by the people who work in them on a one member, one vote system. Profits are ploughed back into the business in order to expand or create more jobs, or the money is used to help set up other community businesses or to provide help in other ways for the local community. No one gets a personal financial share from the business's profits.

Consider whether there are ways in which *your* local community could be better served through improved local provision. Talk to people about your ideas. Stir up some common interest. If there are no businesses out there interested in investing in your area, then you can certainly start the ball rolling by taking things into your own collective hands and setting up your own community business. It may start off by employing only a handful of people, but that is still an important handful, especially if one of them is you.

Because the aim of this type of venture is not to make profit for profit's sake, or for the sake of shareholders, finding the start-up costs can be difficult through normal channels. However, many local authorities are keen to support local initiatives, especially if they help not only to reduce unemployment, but also generate surplus profits which can be ploughed back into the community. Contact your local town hall's Economic Development Unit (it may go by another name in your area). There may be special government grants available if you live in a particularly deprived area, and you could also apply for funding from:

- Your local Training & Enterprise Council (TEC) or Local Enterprise Company (LEC); addresses in the telephone directory, or from your local Job Centre.
- Grant-making trusts (see the Directory of Grant-Making Trusts in your reference library).

- The European Social Fund (contact your local authority, or Citizen's Advice Bureau to find out how applications are organized in your locality).
- Large businesses may be able to offer money or help in kind eg office equipment, advice, use of facilities and so on.
- Local organizations may also be able to offer help in kind eg colleges, voluntary organizations, Chambers of Commerce etc.

By now you may be convinced that creating your own employment is definitely the way forward. I hope so. But it will obviously need more than good intentions. In the space available it isn't possible to go into the finer details of how you go about actually setting up in business, but there are many good books available, to get you thinking. High street banks also have free information packs about going into business. Call in and ask for a copy. Or hire the video *Community Enterprise in Action* from the Community Development Foundation. You may be eligible to go on an enterprise training course; ask at your Job Centre about local training provision. A course like that would equip you with the basic skills you need to help you set up in business. In the meantime, here are a few more pointers:

Community Development Foundation
60 Highbury Grove
London N5 2AG
Tel. 071 226 5375

▪ IDEAS

You may have the enthusiasm but are lacking in business ideas. These suggestions may help:

- Buy a viable existing business (*Dalton's Weekly* carries advertisements of businesses for sale).

- Learning new skills on a training course can give you lots of ideas about business possibilities.
- Go to your library; have a look at books like *101 Ways to Start Your Own Business* by yours truly, Christine Ingham.
- Talk to people.
- Consider whether a franchise might be a possibility ie buying a business blueprint from an established franchisor who also provides on-going training and support in exchange for a percentage share of your profits. Contact the British Franchise Association.
- Look at what you personally have to offer.
- Look at what is needed in your local or surrounding area.
- Look around at what potential is waiting to be realized, either in places, people, or things.

British Franchise Association
Thames View
Newtown Road
Henley-on-Thames
Oxon RG9 1HG
Tel. 0491 578049

Whatever you decide on, make sure it is something in which your heart is one hundred per cent. With all the hard work involved, you will need that belief and love of what you're doing to help you carry on when the going gets tough.

• MARKET RESEARCH

When you have settled on one or two ideas, you must do your market research. Basically, this means making sure there really is a market for your wonderful new brandy-flavoured cottage cheese! You might love it, but will others buy it? How will you find your customers? How will they find out about you? You really have to test out your idea fully. In the long run it will save you making very costly mistakes, and will also lend credibility to applications for loans if you can say that your research shows there really is a gap in the market for this wonderful new delicacy — and people are clamouring to buy it.

· COSTINGS

Work out how much it will cost you to make your product or deliver your service. Include *all* overheads, right down to the last paper clip. Then work out how much you will have to charge in order to make a profit. Does it seem feasible?

· MONEY

Raising the money to start off your venture depends on so many things, not least of which is whether you intend to work on your own, or join forces in a co-operative venture or a community business. But if you are going solo, here are a few suggestions:

- You can start some enterprises with little more than a willing heart, such as offering to do odd jobs for people. There is no need to sign-off if you are claiming Unemployment Benefit or Income Support, but you must declare your earnings. Once you exceed the earnings limit, you will have it deducted from your benefits, but so long as you can still prove that you are also available for and actively seeking employment, it shouldn't be much of a problem (see page 25). If in doubt, ask to speak to someone about how your benefits would be affected if you did the occasional job for someone. In this way you can build up your business and work towards being totally free of benefits.
- Apply to go on the Enterprise Allowance Scheme which now varies from area to area. Some offer £50 a week

during the first year of business while others offer greater or smaller amounts for shorter or longer periods of time. Your local TEC, LEC or Job Centre will have details. TECs and LECs will also have details of other funds for which you may be eligible to apply, so DO ASK. You may also still be eligible for some Income Support if your earnings as a self-employed person are low. Ask at your local Social Security office or dial Freephone 0800 666555.

• Enquire at your local town hall's Economic Development Unit for details of grants and enterprise funding schemes in your area.

• Ask friends and relatives if they would be interested in investing in your business.

• If you live in an old coal-mining or steel-producing area, there may be additional funds, help and support available; contact British Coal Enterprise Ltd or British Steel Industry.

British Coal Enterprise Ltd
60 Station Road
Sutton-in-Ashfield
Notts NG17 5GA
Tel. 0623 442244

British Steel Industry
Bridge House
Bridge Street
Sheffield S3 8NS
Tel. 0742 731612

• Find a private investor. Solicitors, accountants, stockbrokers and possibly banks may have customers who have private funds to invest in new businesses.

• Contact your Local Enterprise Trust. Your local TEC or LEC should have details.

• Do you have any assets you could sell, or could you

modify your personal circumstances to free up some cash to start you off?

- Don't let money be an obstacle to your commitment. If you are truly committed to your vision and it is one which is aligned with your real life's aim, your reason for being here, your 'bliss' (ie if your intuition tells you it feels right), then money and support will come to you.

Creating your own work can be incredibly demanding, but it can also be immensely rewarding. It could be the opportunity which is presenting itself to you through being unemployed. Working for yourself is a chance for you to realize your own power, your own abilities and enthusiasms, and not least of all, your own vision.

8 ▪ *Help Others; Help Yourself*

Besides money, there are a lot of things which seem to disappear when you are unemployed: feeling as though you have something useful to do with your time; feeling that you matter and are of some importance; feeling that there is a manageable challenge in your life. What takes their place is constant reinforcement that: without a job there isn't anything to do (or anything you want to do; all those chores you never got around to doing before are not going to look any more attractive to you now); all the rejection letters from unsuccessful job applications tell you that you are of no importance; the only challenges in your life appear unmanageable and seem to depend on the whims of others. In the meantime, your skills, experience and enthusiasm is slowly being drained away with yet another week without work.

Voluntary work may help to bring a halt to these difficulties, and it certainly brings a whole range of benefits, not only to the community but also to yourself. It is not a reasonable or desirable substitute for paid employment, if that is what you want, but working as a volunteer can bring you as much, if not more, fulfilment as a regular nine-to-five job would. But I do believe that, as with most things, it should come from the heart. Being forced to do 'voluntary work' in exchange for benefits takes that vital element out of the whole equation. Doing something purely for money's sake is entirely different and has a completely different energy around it from doing something quite simply because you want to.

▪ THE BENEFITS TO YOU

Few of us are one hundred per cent altruistic. We like to know what we can get out of a situation, especially if we are possibly going to put in some hard graft in exchange. So, what's in it for you?

Voluntary work provides you with an opportunity:

- To practice your skills and keep them 'live' to an acceptable standard. It will help convince potential employers that although you haven't had a paid job, you haven't lost your valuable expertise — and enthusiasm.
- To keep your CV 'live' by providing you with useful work experience which makes the best use of your existing skills.
- To increase your chances of finding a job. The more you network, the greater the possibility of hearing about a vacancy before it gets advertised.
- To start to develop a sense of purposefulness, other than that of job hunting, and to build a structure to your day or week which revolves around more than signing on and cashing in the Giro.
- To make contact with a whole new range of people and possibly to make friends. This is another vital element which people so dearly miss through being unemployed.
- To gain new experiences. New experiences make us feel more alive and give us energy. Being without them tends to lead to feelings of stagnation and decline.
- To feel useful again. Constant negative reinforcement can lead us to feel that we are worth nothing, because others seem to keep telling us this. We all need to feel useful. We all *are* useful.
- To distract us away from constantly worrying about our own problems around money, family difficulties, job hunting etc. This isn't to encourage you to ignore them; simply to take them out of the limelight for a while and to give you a breather. Immersing your energies into other activities can help you see your own problems from a new perspective.
- To get out of the house! With little cash to spare even for additional bus fares, getting out and about can be nigh on impossible. This can be a most welcome opportunity to get away from the same four walls for a while.

- To try out a new occupation. After reassessing your career and life aims, you may have decided on an alternative. Work as a volunteer could provide you with experience in your new chosen field, without having to risk all, to see if you like it.
- To combat any feelings of depression and isolation which you may have been experiencing. Getting out and about and actually getting involved can be a great help.
- To develop a new career.

And talking of benefits . . .

If you do take up any voluntary work, you must tell them when you sign on. You should have no difficulties so long as:

- The payments you receive from doing any voluntary work are for expenses only eg reimbursement of travel expenses.
- Payments *in addition* to reimbursement of expenses do not exceed the amounts you are allowed to earn in a week. (See page 25.)
- You do not commit yourself to working full time for a definite period. It may be seen that you are no longer available for work and your benefits might be forfeited; but so long as you are available for and actively seeking work, even though you are taking part in voluntary work, you should be fine.

Working as a volunteer should not leave you out of pocket.

▪ WHAT'S AVAILABLE

There is a vast range of ways in which you can contribute. Here are just a few to give you some idea of the scope of opportunities available to you:

- Fundraising — helping to organize and run events, working on the administrative side, or simply doing your bit on flag days. At a higher level, it might be worth noting that some national charities pay top salaries for fund-raisers. Could this provide the way you've been looking for to make a career change?

- Campaigning — either to raise the general profile of an organization and bring it to the attention of the people who matter, or campaigning over a specific issue.
- Shop work — helping out in charity shops.
- Office work — typing, answering the phone, working on mail shots etc.
- Befriending — making regular contact with people who may not have many opportunities to socialize eg people with learning difficulties, people who are older and living on their own, people with disabilities.
- Advocacy — more than just befriending, an advocate helps people to speak up for themselves and ensures they receive all the help and support to which they are entitled, but which they would otherwise have difficulty in accessing. Advocacy schemes are particularly of help to people with learning difficulties.
- General help — an extra pair of willing hands can be most welcome. It might appeal to you if you are happy simply doing whatever needs to be done, without limiting yourself to any one particular job. Obviously there will be lots of variety in this sort of work.
- Using existing skills — practically any skills you might have can be put to some use in some sort of voluntary capacity: story-telling skills, accountancy or book-keeping skills, managerial skills, photographic skills, listening skills, writing skills, DIY skills. Think about what you have to offer and which you and others could benefit from by putting into practice.
- Organizing — special events such as an arts, music or other sort of festival.
- Learning new skills — you may receive training in order to help you carry out the voluntary work.

- Counselling — if you are a good listener, you could put these skills to good use by becoming a counsellor.

This should give you some indication of the wide range of activities and possibilities. Similarly there are lots of different settings in which you could work and groups of people or organizations you could become involved with. Here are a few examples:

- British Trust for Conservation Volunteers

- Your local wildlife trust

- RSPCA

- Greenpeace

- Relate (formerly the Marriage Guidance Council)

- Victim support work

- The Samaritans

- Hospitals:
    - DJ-ing on the hospital radio service
    - offering beauty care to long-stay patients
    - visiting people who are on their own
    - helping to run the trolley shop
    - helping to run the mobile library

- Luncheon clubs

- Prison visiting

- Supporting ex-prisoners

- Adult literacy classes

- People with disabilities

- Playgroups

- St John's Ambulance

- Mountain rescue
- Children's homes
- Elderly people, at home or in residential care
- The National Trust
- Day centres
- Voluntary Service Overseas (see page 36).

Also, check on any government schemes for people who are unemployed. Currently the Employment Action scheme finds places with charities for people who have existing skills to offer. Benefits are not affected, travel expenses are reimbursed, *and* you receive an additional £10 a week. You are also provided with time in which to continue with your job search activities. Ask for details at your local Job Centre.

Obviously the list above is by no means fully comprehensive. There are lots of other charities, voluntary organizations and community groups which would dearly welcome your offer of help. There may also be local initiatives specific to your area.

▪ FINDING OUT MORE

First of all, have a think about the sort of work you would like to do and the fields in which you are most interested. For voluntary work to be successful it is important that you concentrate on the areas you feel most comfortable and happiest with. If you find children a trial, it would be foolish to consider working in a children's home. Although you might have the best intentions, your heart wouldn't be in the work — and it would eventually show. However, if you feel a certain empathy with the environment, then direct your efforts towards voluntary work where you can help clear ditches, plant trees or clean up canals. Whatever you do, decide on something that your heart really is in. Voluntary work isn't a sentence — it's something to be enjoyed.

There may be a volunteer bureau in your area. If so, this will be your first port of call. The Citizens Advice Bureau will also keep lists of local organizations which use volunteers, as may local colleges. Requests for help may be posted on your local community notice board or in the library, as well as in the local press or on radio. Keep a look out. You could also call in to charity shops in person, or visit offices where local charities are based, and if, for example, you would like to help out in a hospital or work with elderly people in residential care, go along and find out what sort of voluntary help is currently needed and who organizes it. They may also be able to provide you with other useful leads. Failing that, the Volunteer Centre UK has a database which holds volunteering opportunities throughout the country. Contact: The Volunteer Centre UK, 29 Lower King's Road, Berkhamsted, Herts, HP4 2AB. Tel: 0442 870852. They can also provide names and addresses of organizations you may wish to contact. You may also want to look through the *Directory of Volunteer and Employment Opportunities*, or *A Practical Guide to Volunteer and Employment Opportunities* by Jan Brownfoot and Frances Wilks, both published by the Directory of Social Change. Ask your library for copies.

If you know which organization you want to work for, simply find their address either from the volunteer bureau who can tell you if there is a local branch, from the telephone directory or from your local library, and contact them direct. The Volunteer Centre can also help with addresses.

▪ BUT THERE'S NOTHING AVAILABLE

You may find that after researching into what is available in your area that you come up with nothing more than a blank zero. Or, you may have identified a gap in provision for a particular group of people. If that's the case you've just stumbled on a golden opportunity — to set up a volunteer scheme yourself! Here's your chance to gain lots of excellent experience, stretch your skills and abilities, and take on a real challenge. What you learn in the process could stand you in good stead for later setting up a more commercial enterprise. Certainly it will help enliven your CV.

As with any enterprise you need to do lots of groundwork and research. You have identified a perceived gap in the market, but is there a *real* need for the provision you have in mind? You can only find out by talking to people about it, both the people who would be using the service and other professionals in the field. If all looks well, start to consider the types of people you need to help run the scheme and the skills you would like them to bring. You may be able to get enough people to form a steering group by trawling among your friends and acquaintances. It might also be worth considering recruiting a local person with a high public profile to give their patronage to the group, or even a local business to help sponsor it. If you find you need to advertise for members be prepared for more offers than expected, especially since replying to everyone would generate a lot of expense for you. Perhaps this contingency could be provided for through careful wording of your advertisement.

Even though you may have never run a meeting before, it will inevitably be your responsibility to chair the first one. It needn't be very formal, just well organized to make sure that you get through the business in hand. Make a list beforehand. You will want to clarify what your objectives are, appoint a chairperson and secretary, consider the recruitment of volunteers, and work out how to find potential users of the service. You will probably need a few meetings before you can get properly underway and at some stage the thorny issue of funding will be raised.

Raising funds in order to get the project off the ground may be your first priority; this is where the good old jumble sales, coffee mornings and sponsored events come into their own (although you could try to think up something more original).

You could also consider what local authority funds may be available, as well as drawing up a list of local businesses which may be able to offer donations and support. You could ask them for donations of furniture, equipment, services (such as use of their photocopier), manpower or money. Don't be shy — just ask. You'll probably be pleasantly surprised at just how helpful people are when they can see it is for charity (much nicer than when you ask them for a job!). Further afield, the *Directory of Grant-Making Trusts*, published by the Charities Aid Foundation and which can be found in reference libraries lists bodies to which you may be eligible to apply for funds, or consult the two volumes of *A Guide to the Major Trusts*, published by The Directory of Social Change who also publish a set of fundraising leaflets.

Directory of Social Change
Radius Works
Back Lane
London NW3 1HL
Tel. 071 284 4364

In the early stages, you may be comfortable working from a kitchen table at home. When things become a bit busier and you suddenly realize there's nowhere to eat your cornflakes in the morning, accommodation will have to be put onto the agenda. You may be able to find a disused garage, a corner in a building (eg church, youth club, town hall, other charity) or some other place to use as your base. Spend some time putting the feelers out to see what free space you can come up with — again you might be pleasantly surprised. But if you do draw a blank, see if your local authority has a listing of property available on cheap, short-term lets which your funding might allow you to make use of — or see what the volunteer bureau has to suggest.

Obviously this only scratches the surface of what's involved in setting up a voluntary project. It would be worthwhile talking to other existing organizations, who work in a similar field. Find out how they operate and be willing to learn from their experience and expertise. They may be able to come up with useful suggestions to help you get off the ground or names of people who could help. The Volunteer Centre UK has a useful list of publications and may also be of help.

> The Volunteer Centre UK
> 29 Lower King's Road
> Berkhamsted
> Herts HP4 2AB
> Tel. 0442 870852

The fulfilment you can get from becoming involved in voluntary work can be enormous, and from setting up a project from scratch even more so. And although it will not provide you with the salary you need, it may well provide you with all the other vital elements, and more, that a regular job would be able to. It may even be a way which could lead you, indirectly, towards other employment opportunities. Volunteering is no longer about do-gooding by the upper or middle classes. Volunteering is about helping yourself by helping others.

9 ▪ *Joining In – Where the Action Is*

It is so easy to look at being employed through rose tints when you're out of work. It seems to be so desirable, so much what we want, that we forget we probably day-dreamed on a regular basis about that one glorious day when we wouldn't have to work any more, when we could call our time our own, when we wouldn't have The Boss constantly telling us what to do. Now you have the time, somehow those day-dreams seem to have been forgotten amid the difficulties of trying to come to terms with the new, albeit perhaps temporary, change in lifestyle.

When you are in work life tends to centre around the dictates of a job, where social activities tend to be limited to costly leisure pursuits which we use like tranquillizers to calm us down after the hectic schedule of combining work and family life. You certainly don't seem to have much free time when you're working — barely enough to wash your socks in! Gradually many people can come to feel that although their belly is full, there's a curious empty quality to their life; it feels impoverished somehow. The knock-on effect is seen in our neighbourhoods and communities which begin to degenerate from the lack of real involvement by its residents. There just isn't the time. Let's just go down the pub instead. Let's leave it to the council to sort out. Our lives become narrow, blinkered, limited. Fortunately being unemployed can rescue us from that pattern.

Now is a time when you can take up the opportunity to start joining in again — or perhaps even for the first time. It can start to bring you into contact, not only with your community or locality, but also with your own personal self. It can help you start to put some life back into your community, your household, your own life.

Without the regular contact with people which being in a

job provides, it is easy to experience feelings of isolation. Or if you're younger, and haven't yet been in work, you might begin to find that old school friends start to drift away from the area, perhaps to get married, go to college, or to start work; and your own family may be making noises about it being time you left the fledgling nest, too. Feelings of isolation are distressing and difficult to cope with, and somehow rubbing shoulders with people down at the Job Centre or in the dole queue just doesn't quite solve the problem. And in looking around it may seem to you that a glass wall separates you from all those others who are in work and who are off to have a good time. You have nothing to do because you haven't a job, haven't the money and can't join them at the cinema. It all adds to those feelings of isolation, and once you start to focus on that it is difficult to see all those other wonderful opportunities for joining in which are just waiting for you to explore and which may give you lots more fulfilment than just hanging out with your mates again at the Hope and Anchor (or whatever your equivalent might be).

Joining in generates a feeling of belonging, and breaks through that sense of isolation. As with volunteering it also provides a way in which to start building structure into your life; one which relieves the monotony of job hunting, job hunting and more job hunting. Through breaking into that monotonous cycle, a new rhythm is created which adds a sense of aliveness and light-heartedness to your life. The new experiences you encounter bring novelty back into your life and start to broaden horizons which might have been in danger of reaching no further than from here to the next rejection letter. As more interests are taken up, you start to feel the spark again, and it shows — we suddenly become more interesting people to others. And as they respond to us, we in turn find them more interesting, too. You're on the upward spiral. Energy starts to flow through, and even the latent energies in the anger and frustration you may have been feeling can now be released creatively and put to good use.

On the more practical side, the more people you meet and

mix with always increases your chances of making use of those informal networks through which the majority of vacancies are filled. You may have little in common with Ms Business-woman other than being in the same interest group, but she could be the one who tips you off when she hears on the grapevine of a job coming up, giving you a head start on all the other applicants. Also, you might find that joining in provides ideas for spin-offs into creating your own employment, either by yourself or with others (see Chapter 7).

• WHAT DOES IT ALL MEAN?

You may well be wondering what is actually meant by 'joining in'; what sort of commitment are we talking about; is it all about church gatherings and school fêtes? The answer is: only if you want it to be. As with all other things, the benefits to yourself will only come about through listening to, and answering your own needs. Let them dictate the sort of joining in you do. In that way you will find yourself moving closer towards your true life path and when you do so you will start to feel real fulfilment, perhaps more than any job you've applied for could ever give you.

Spend some time thinking about what sort of person you are and what you want 'joining in' to mean to you. It will obviously reflect your own personal interests, but beyond that you may be someone who wants to join a group which is geared towards physical action in some way, or on the other hand you may prefer more passivity, in which case 'joining in' to you might mean attending lectures or talks. You can even achieve a sense of involvement just through receiving regular newsletters from organizations, keeping you in touch with what's happening in your particular field of interest. For more involvement you may want the opportunity to practice skills and develop particular interests, or you may want to join in as a way of finding out more about something.

Joining in offers a way to feel more part of the community.

This may be the predominant need which you want it to serve. On the other hand you may simply just want to be with more people, or find support through contact with others. Or then again, you may want to become an active member, who wants to find an opportunity to come in from the sidelines of life for a while. We are all individuals with our own complex needs. Spend some time considering what yours are and what you want joining in to mean to you.

▪ WHAT'S AVAILABLE

Opportunities will vary from area to area, but hopefully these suggestions will at least provide a springboard for your own thoughts, ideas and research:

Pressure Groups

National organizations like Greenpeace or Amnesty International may have, or be wanting to set up, a local branch. There may also be local groups concerned with issues specific to your area, such as improving public transport for people with disabilities, or saving a piece of land from developers. Your local newspaper should give you some ideas.

Adult Education Classes

A whole range of different classes and short courses are organized by local adult education colleges, and not all of them are academically focused. Have a look at their prospectus to see what's on offer. Most offer concessionary rates.

Political Groups

If you don't like the way the nation is being run, you could start to do something about it by joining in and becoming an active member of a political party. I decided to join in a while ago and soon had my time filled with duties around the ward in which I live. Whichever party you have sympathies with, I'm sure they'd like to hear from you. Addresses of local party headquarters should be available from your local library or town hall. You could also attend open debates held by your local council which provide a real opportunity to have your voice heard. Keep an eye on the town hall's notice board.

Community Activities

You can join in and help out at regular events on your local calendar such as fêtes, arts festivals and bank holiday celebrations, or become involved with the more on-going and established regular activities like running the local youth club. Watch your local press for details, or try to find out who's in charge of organizing the events. The town hall or Citizen's Advice Bureau may be a good start.

Campaigning on Local Issues

If you feel strongly about a local issue and there is already a group involved in campaigning about it I'm sure they would like your support in whatever form it takes. And if there isn't a group addressing an issue which is of concern to you, get one going. (Read on to Chapter 10.)

Pen-friends

In a more distant, though still feasible way, you can join in through contact with pen-friends, both at home and abroad. Special interest magazines and national newspapers often carry personal advertisements for pen-friends, or you could ask for help from church leaders or local branches of national organizations to help you arrange something.

Charities

Local and national charities are always on the look-out for willing souls, and you may get your expenses reimbursed. (Read Chapter 8.)

Mothers' Groups

Often a vital link with sanity, mothers' groups can be a real help to those who join. If there isn't one in your area, why not start one?

Women's Institute

Don't knock it till you've tried it. Women's Institutes aren't all thick stockings and jam recipes. Go along and see what your local branch has to offer, perhaps armed with an idea of what you can offer it, too. Addresses from your local library or Citizens Advice Bureau.

Unemployed Centre

If you're fortunate enough there may be a local drop-in centre for people who are unemployed. This can be of real help and provide valuable support, not least of all through meeting other people who are having similar experiences to yourself. And what a comfort that can be, just to know you're not alone in what you are going through. They can also be a vital source of information and help. Joining in could mean making use of the facilities, or it could mean being more actively involved in the running of it.

Religious Groups

Whatever your faith, you may benefit from joining in activities based around your religion. Again, a willing pair of hands to help organize or run activities is often more than welcome.

Ask what's available. They may also run classes, groups and activities which you never knew about and which are just what you've been looking for.

Sporting/Fitness Groups

You always promised yourself that some day you really would embark on that fitness routine. Now is as good a time as any. See what's available at your local sports centre, swimming pool, YMCA, adult education college, church, or any other centre which you think might offer what you want. Also, contact the Leisure Department at your town hall to see what's available. And if there isn't the cycling group you were hoping to find, why not start one going? I'm sure there are a few other disappointed people who would welcome someone taking the initiative.

Creative Groups

Music, art, drama, writing, literature. Whatever your interest you could benefit enormously by joining a local group. Being in a job makes it difficult to find time to express our creative abilities, so take advantage of the opportunity you have now. Your local college or library should have details of what's on in your area. And again, if there's nothing happening where you live, that's a good opportunity for you to start the ball rolling. A shared enthusiasm is enough to make the group a riotous success.

Esoteric Groups

There seems to be a gradual awakening within people to the more spiritual (and by that I don't mean religious) sides to our lives. Thank goodness. With the hurly-burly cut and thrust of life with a job, it can be almost impossible to listen to the small voice of our more spiritual sides crying for its needs to be met. This is perhaps the best opportunity yet which being unemployed brings. Visit your local library to see what books they have; check the notice board in health food shops to see if any groups are advertised; buy (or have a look at in the shops or library) magazines like *Prediction* or *Resurgence*.

Environmental

Realize your chance to do something positive for the environment. You don't have to have green fingers, just a willing heart, or simply join in the local debate on environmental issues. Contact Greenpeace or Friends of the Earth, or ask at your local library for information about other local environmental organizations.

Greenpeace UK
Canonbury Villas
London N1 2PN
Tel. 071 354 5100

Friends of the Earth
26–28 Underwood Street
London N1 7JQ
Tel. 071 490 1555

Schools

There are always lots of opportunities to join in and help with school activities, whether it's having your voice heard at PTA meetings, becoming a school governor, or just running a stall at the Christmas jumble sale.

Jobclub

Joining one of the government-sponsored Job Clubs apparently significantly increases your chance of finding a job. Feeling part of a team, it can provide you with a welcome boost of support to flagging job search activities. Ask at your local Job Centre for details.

In Uniform

There are opportunities to join in if you would like to play an active role in supporting the police force or the armed forces. You could enquire at your local police station about becoming a Special Constable, or consider joining the Territorial Army.

> Territorial Army
> Duke of York's HQ
> Chelsea
> London SW3
> Tel. 071 730 8131

Of course, there are probably many other sorts of groups and activities which may be available in your local area for you to join. There may also be those clubs which are advertised in special interest journals or magazines and which are just what you're looking for, if you prefer less directly involved activities. Keep your eyes open.

Addresses and contacts for either local or national organizations can be found through a number of sources, which can also provide you with more ideas about what is available:

- Your local library
- Citizens Advice Bureau
- Local church or other religious centre
- Community centre
- Community worker
- Local newspaper
- People — ask them what they're involved in; tell them what you're interested in; ask them if they have any suggestions.

Skill shares, social clubs, gardening clubs, stamp clubs, scrabble, chess, bridge, orienteering, mah-jong, you name it and there is probably a club or group devoted to it, and just waiting to be discovered by you. And if there isn't, there is absolutely nothing which says you can't be the person who starts one going. It only needs you to find a few like-minded souls, then the rest of the work involved in setting up a group is shared out between members, so there's no need to feel that you wouldn't be up to it. You wouldn't have to run the operation — unless you wanted to. All you need to do is find the people to join in with you. The rest is easy. Read on to the next chapter for more information.

Although it is individuals who experience unemployment, its effect is mirrored and seen throughout whole communities, from the local neighbourhood right through to whole towns and beyond. It starts with a person feeling depressed at their situation and seemingly hopeless future; they feel powerless at their seeming inability to make any progress because decisions that affect them always appear to be taken by others; they feel rejected because no one seems to want what they have to offer; they feel angry at the frustration caused through the culmination of all this.

What the individual experiences on the personal level eventually becomes reflected in the environment at large. And so neighbourhoods and communities look and feel depressed; there is no energy in them; no spirit. They go into decline because there is no one who seems to want to revitalize them by accessing the latent power within them. They look rejected, uncared for; no one wants them any more, especially if they have been built around single industries or employers who have since abandoned them. And the areas are a witness to the anger which, perhaps understandably, finds a release through smashing windows, vandalism, crime.

It becomes a vicious circle. Living in such an environment makes you feel even worse, and so the environment becomes worse. But where will it all end? Bureaucrats throwing money at it rarely brings any long-term change or benefit to the community; but then money rarely solves underlying problems. The answer can't come from the environment, which in this context is inert, and so it must come from the other element in the situation: the individual.

The individual has it within his or her power to change things for the better. *You* have the power to change things for the better; for yourself and for your community. From the breakdown of old forms as they were, new ones emerge. Imagine a star shooting up and across the heavens, glowing brightly, but which then suddenly explodes and bursts, just like our personal hopes and dreams over the last few years or so. Yet if you look more closely at the sky after the explosion you will see that falling down gently is a shower of star-dust; a sparkling glitter through whose sweeps and swirls we can just about see, if we look carefully, the shapes, outlines and intimations of new things to come.

So if you feel that no one cares about what becomes of your community, let alone you as an individual; if you feel that the council or the politicians couldn't care a hoot, then now is the time for the only person who does care, to start the ball rolling: you. Instead of waiting for things to happen (and it could be a very long wait, given the present economic climate) you can *make* it happen. You can start to make things transform into the way you want them to be.

As an individual, or as a member of a group, you can start to reclaim your power from the remote hands of 'Others' by transforming the energies of frustration and anger into positive action. You can use it to change and rebuild the local economy, and more fundamentally the local spirit. You don't need to have money to do it, but you do need the enthusiasm to want to change things for the better in your life. And in the process you will discover more about yourself, your community and the other people who live in it. You will learn new skills and perhaps surprise yourself as you meet and manage new challenges. By putting your energies into action in order to change things you care about and which affect you and your life, you will feel a new sense of commitment, a sense of excitement as developments take place, a thrill as successes are achieved. You will become an active participant, making a difference to things. Your effect will be felt. Your belief in yourself will start to grow and so will your self-esteem.

None of this is new. Individuals up and down the UK and beyond have been making things happen in their communities for years. Since time began, individuals have taken the initiative and realized the latent power which we all have within us. Unfortunately society tends to make us forget our own, but now it is your turn to discover yours.

You may already have an initiative you would like to get off the ground, and be half way to doing it in your mind's eye. Most of us are rather more reticent and shy. It is normally 'other people' who put things into action. And if you have been unemployed for a while, confidence is going to be low and you'll probably already be thinking that you couldn't possibly do anything like that — helping to get a community off the ground. But you can. And if you don't, I wonder who will? There are probably a mass of people living nearby who, like you, are angry and concerned and also reticent, shy, lacking in confidence and who are waiting for someone else to make the first move. And that is perhaps all you will have to do. It just needs someone to say something first; like at those awful parties where everyone stands around looking embarrassed, until someone says something; anything will do to provide the hook for others to pick up on. Starting an action group to get things moving needs much the same.

So, assuming you want others to join in, think about how you can get them interested. It may be useful firstly to consider what members of the group could have in common to give it its identity. Here are some suggestions:

- Neighbourhood
- Local community
- Religion
- Culture
- Language
- Age
- Gender
- Common experience eg single parenthood, unemployment, disability, low incomes
- Members of an already established group, even a local branch of a national organization.

You may be able to identify others within your area. Group identities provide a common bond which is vital in getting people's commitment to making things happen.

Really there is no limit to the sorts of issues you may want to address. It may be something relatively simple, or something incredibly complex and ambitious. Whatever you feel strongly enough about is where your energy lies, waiting to be put to good use. If there is anything you feel would improve the quality of your life, and the lives of others, then go for it. If it seems like it's a case of 'Frankly, everything needs changing', and you feel like bull-dozing the lot, here are a few suggestions to help focus the mind a bit better and perhaps provide material for discussion:

Advice

Would you like somewhere where you could go to receive *real* help and advice about benefits, debt, housing, welfare rights etc?

Tenants Association

Do you think more could be done about the quality of your housing and immediate neighbourhood if there were a group to put things into action? Perhaps it could help to revitalize community activities, too.

Counselling

Being unemployed brings with it not only practical problems but also feelings of additional stresses and strains. Perhaps a counselling service would benefit you and others and help support people as they work through those feelings of depression, hopelessness, even despair.

Fun

Is there enough affordable fun in your locale? Is there enough entertainment for children, youngsters, families, elderly people? Would you like to see people enjoying themselves actually within the community? Would you like to be able to have fun without it costing half of next week's dole money?

Health

Would you like to feel healthier? Is there a particular health issue in your area which you would like to see addressed eg chest complaints in children, HIV?

Cafe

Would you like to have somewhere to go to socialize on an informal basis; somewhere to get out of the house to for a while, without it costing much? Can you see how your community might benefit from such a place, run as a community business or on a co-operative basis?

Child Care/Play Activities

If you're a parent who experiences difficulties because of a lack of adequate child care or play facilities, perhaps others might like to help organize something on a local level and share with you in the benefits.

Crime

When the spirit of a neighbourhood starts to die, crime has a loop-hole through which to creep in. If this has happened where you live and you are worried about it, your neighbours will probably be feeling the same too. If you no longer feel safe where you live, band together with others and decide what is to be done about it.

Campaign on Local Issues

You and your neighbours are the best people to see what needs changing, where. Moans and groans about longed-for improvements might make you feel better, but won't change anything. Think about what you'd like to change: an improved bus service; improved facilities for people with disabilities; establishing a community centre; expanding the range of goods and services offering concessionary rates; traffic problems; drug problems.

National Campaign Issues

Your energies need not be confined to solely local issues. If you feel passionate about wanting changes to things like the benefit system or age discrimination, you can still take action. You might like to see if there is a national organization for which you could establish a local branch.

Enterprise Initiatives

Areas improve with thriving local economies. Talk to others about your ideas for wanting to bring business into the area and improve employment opportunities, perhaps through establishing community businesses, co-operatives or self-employment (see Chapter 7, and below). People elsewhere have done it successfully, and there are probably lots of people willing to give it a try who live quite close by.

Training

There is probably a wealth of under-used talent within walking distance from where you live. There are people who are retired, enthusiastic amateurs, people who have acquired a vast range of knowledge etc. All this could benefit others within the community if the skills could be passed on through formal or informal training — if someone got the ball going . . . .

Arts Project

If you feel that graffiti is the cry for a creative outlet, and that the only drama highlight in the year is the school nativity play, you might want to think about the potential for developing an arts project to liven up not only the environment but also people's creative spirit. Or you might prefer to do something more individualistic (or in a group) and make a television programme. For example, the BBC's *Open Space* slot enables members of the public to make a television programme which is completely under their own editorial control. They provide all the technical back-up, you provide the idea and work alongside the programme makers. It can provide you with the opportunity to put across your own personal viewpoint on an issue, 'educate' or even 're-educate' people about something which touches your life, or about an experience which you have had. Initially you only need to submit a proposal which briefly sketches out your ideas. Their leaflet 'Access in Action with the BBC Community Programme Unit' explains more.

Community Programme Unit
39 Wales Farm Road
London W3 6XJ
Tel. 081 743 8000 x 3500

Environmental

Fed up with the way your area looks? Derelict buildings? Waste land? Sitting there are golden opportunities just waiting to be exploited. The buildings could be refurbished to provide cheap workspace for people wanting to start their own enterprises; be turned into the community space you've been looking for; be the ideal place for a youth centre or community cafe. Similarly, the waste land could be landscaped, turned into a city farm, made into allotments, become a cycle track, etc.

These suggestions will, I hope, provide a springboard for

your own ideas. Here are also a few other specific suggestions which may be of particular benefit to your community:

Food Bulk Buy

A large percentage of people's weekly money is spent on food. Large supermarkets may be cheaper, but transport can be a problem and adds cost back on since new stores are inevitably built on the outskirts of town where walking access can be difficult. On the other hand local, smaller shops may be more convenient but are also more expensive. They may be the only option for some people. Running along the co-operative lines (see page 77), a food bulk-buying service helps by passing on the savings which have been made from having bought in bulk to the customers, ie you. It also cuts your transport costs and improves access, since the service is normally run from a local centre such as a community or church hall. Where shops have to build mark-ups into the prices of goods on the shelf in order to cover staff wages, a bulk-buying co-op is run by volunteers who are members of the scheme, thus keeping prices as low as possible.

Not only is this scheme of direct benefit to individuals in terms of saving money, it also helps the local economy by keeping money circulating within the community for longer before it eventually leaves. It also provides the members who are active in setting up and running the scheme with the chance to develop new skills which may improve employment prospects.

There could be initial resistance from local shops if it looks like their livelihood could be affected; this needs careful consideration. If your service can prove to be a complementary one, so much the better. For further details of how to go about setting up a bulk-buying scheme in your area, contact your local Co-operative Development Agency or the Industrial Common Ownership Movement (see page 78).

Credit Union

Banks have lately received a lot of bad press about their conduct, particularly with regard to people and small businesses which fall into debt. If you are excluded from the banking system, from personal choice or otherwise, a credit union may provide the alternative answer.

Credit unions are community based, and although they are not co-operatives as such, are run along similar lines ie run by members on a voluntary basis; one member, one vote operates; dividends are paid to its members. They encourage people to save regularly, provide financial support and are able to offer loans to its members at much below the market rate. Instead of people having to borrow from loan sharks, credit unions can provide the answer to the need for extra cash. Once established, some unions offer to 'take over' people's outstanding loans, pay them off, and then arrange for the new debt which is to the credit union to be paid back at a much lower rate, and in more reasonable instalments, saving people a lot of money — and worry. Credit unions help to put a sense of power and control back into the hands of individuals, and communities.

Another benefit is that they help to keep money within the community for a longer period of time, thus helping the local economy. And through helping individuals avoid the sometimes costly charges of high street banks or other lenders, it keeps even more money in people's own pockets. This in turn helps them feel more in control, better off, happier — which will in turn begin to be reflected in the community.

It only needs between three and five people to run an organizing committee, and for there to be at least 21 members who share a common bond. The 'bond' could be defined as the area where you all live, the place where you worship or the group or club to which you all belong, or some other similar grouping.

You need no special skills to set one up, although in the process you will inevitably learn new ones; ones which could later help you into employment. A Credit Union Development Worker can help you set things up in the initial stages; all you need is the enthusiasm and commitment. If you think you would like to find out more about how to keep more money in your pocket and how to find a more satisfactory way of handling your money, send for a free information pack to the National Federation of Savings and Co-operative Credit Unions.

National Federation of Savings and
Co-operative Credit Unions
Credit Union House
102 Tong Street
Bradford
West Yorkshire BD4 6HD
Tel. 0274 687692

Local Exchange Trading System (LETS)

Lack of money can cause so many difficulties, whether you're in work or not. And yet what is money? It is only a symbol that an exchange of goods or services to an equal value has taken place. What did people do before money became the great be all? They bartered. The LETS system re-introduces this basic idea to local communities except that no direct exchange is involved. For example, imagine that someone repairs your washing machine. You may be in a position to pay them in kind by providing them with some plants for their garden, and a few vegetables from your allotment. But with the LETS system a direct exchange need not take place. Instead, the person who did the repair earns, say ten credits, with which they can 'buy' something from someone else in the system, and you with your washing machine mended are debited with ten credits, which means you are in a position for someone to come to you for ten credits' worth of vegetables or help in their garden. No money ever changes hands. Bliss. The giro goes further, all those jobs which you haven't been able to afford to pay someone for, get done, and you have the benefit of being able to help someone else out. As with the bulk-buying service and credit union, this is another way of enriching the local economy, by keeping the money within it for a longer period of time. In saving on having to buy in costly goods or services from outside the area, there is more left to spend within the local community. It all helps the process along of starting to regenerate and maintain your local area.

Besides the more obvious benefits, a LETS system provides a way in which to increase communication between members of a community. It also helps to increase your own self-value when you can see that someone else wants what you have to offer (and we all have something to offer). It can provide an opportunity to practice and maintain skills, help to overcome debt within the community, and can even help to build a customer base for people wanting to become self-employed. And all this can be achieved without money. No wonder LETS systems are gaining in popularity up and down the country. Can you afford not to have a LETS system in your area, I wonder?

A one-off small membership fee helps to fund start-up costs and it will need someone, or a small group to organize it. A newsletter to members identifies who has what to offer, and a computer program is available to help keep a track of people's 'accounts'. If you would like further information contact LETSLINK.

LETSLINK
61 Woodcock Road
Warminster
Wilts BA12 9DH
Tel. 0985 217871

• Getting Going

It may seem daunting even to think about something like getting an action group going if you have never done anything like this before. But all you need is enthusiasm and the will to want things to change. You don't have to hold a Masters in Business Administration in order to start, or indeed any paper qualifications. What you do need is a vision of how things could be, and you don't need any GCSEs to be able to do that. So first of all have a think about how you would like to see things improved. Don't worry about any details at this stage at all, just let your mind wander and form a picture or idea in your mind of how much better things could be. This isn't wishful thinking; any successful businessperson will tell you that having a vision is the most important thing to have if you are going to make it. It sets your sights and gets your adrenalin going. You may have lots of different ideas emerging, in which case see if they have a common theme — they may all be community businesses in one form or another, or they may all revolve around the younger members of your community. But whatever it is, the 'right' idea will get you excited. You might find that you're smiling to yourself as you imagine it; you might feel like going out there and then and starting to make things happen straight away. But hold on first. Have a chat to other people; find some like-minded others who would like to investigate the possibilities further (be prepared for those miseries who pooh-pooh any positive ideas or suggestions; it's best to avoid those sorts of downers unless they have some genuine observations to make). But even without the support of others, you can still get things off the ground. Unfortunately, a lot of people have such limited imaginations that they find it very difficult to envisage possibilities until they can see something more concrete. When you get further down the line and they can actually see what you're about, perhaps then they might want to join you.

Talk to as many relevant people as possible who might be able to give you ideas, useful comments, suggestions, practical help and advice. Such people might be: community leaders, local councillors, religious leaders, users of an established service, potential users of the new service or people who would benefit from your proposal, relevant voluntary organizations, social services, youth workers, the police, health workers. Make a list of as many people or organizations you think might help, and as you meet each one, ask if they can recommend anyone else you should meet.

The Neighbourhood Initiatives Foundation helps the residents of local communities to identify needs and realize goals. It has a number of excellent packs, including *Getting Self-Propelled; Don't Let Them Waste Your Time* — excellent at inspiring young people and showing in practical terms how to get their own initiatives off the ground — and the *Feasibility Pack* — a pack to help groups identify ideas for local enterprises.

> Neighbourhood Initiatives Foundation
> The Poplars
> Lightmoor
> Telford
> Shropshire TF4 3QN
> Tel. 0952 590777

Go to your local library (a main branch would be best), and ask for any relevant information on your proposed project (for example, they may have case studies of a similar project in another part of town, know of good reference books on the subject, or be able to provide you with the names of national organizations which could help).

The prospect of approaching and meeting professionals may seem daunting if you haven't done this sort of thing before. If you are worried, going along with someone for support can be a great help. But perhaps more important is to keep your vision firmly fixed in your mind, and let your enthusiasm show. Remember too that the people you will be talking to are only that: people. And people love being asked for their 'professional advice' about something. It makes them feel good, so you will probably be pleasantly surprised by how helpful people are when you approach them in this vein.

With as much relevant information as you can gather, you are in a better position to start working out the plan of action in more detail. And as it starts to take shape more firmly in your mind it will also translate into a clearer picture when you talk to others about it. If you haven't formed a group of interested individuals by this stage, you might like to advertise for them. By word of mouth is cheap, so talk to shopkeepers, the person who delivers milk, or collects insurance, and ask them to spread the word for you. A few notices pinned around local noticeboards (or trees) should cost only a few pence, and there may be a local group to which you could make a short address about your ideas and a request for people to join in. You might like to see if you can get a local dignitary to become involved or to endorse the project's aims.

Once you have a small steering group, you can start to spread the workload around, draw up targets and perhaps formulate a timetable of events. Draw on the skills and expertise that each individual has to offer, then with the plan formulated, and a statement of intent drawn up, you are ready to get the scheme off the ground.

▪ FUNDING

Almost inevitably you will have to address the issue of funding. How will you find the money actually to do what you want, when perhaps none of you have anything more than an embarrassing bank balance to show? It can be done.

You will find it easier to attract funds if you can show that your project can eventually contribute to its own running costs in some way. The people with the money will ideally want to see that your group can also generate other funds, either as a direct result of the activity itself (eg community business, credit unions), or through your own fund-raising activities (eg jumble sales, bring and buy, coffee mornings, barbecues, raffles, sponsored events, competitions etc). So bear this is mind in drawing up your plans to show prospective sponsors.

'Funds are very tight', you will inevitably be told more than once, but here are some suggestions of some possible sources:

* Local dignitaries.
* Local businesses, chambers of commerce, trades councils.
* Special local funds eg mayor's fund, Rotary club.
* Local authority; although Urban Aid funding is being cut back, it is still worth enquiring about applying at your town hall. Your area may also have access to City Challenge funds. Special funds may be available in different departments eg youth, environment.
* National bodies eg Sports Council, Arts Council.
* The Government eg through schemes like the Safer Cities project which funds local anti-crime initiatives. See *The Central Government Grants Guide* published by The Directory of Social Change; available through libraries.
* Community Development Foundation; see Chapter 7, page 80.
* Church Action with the Unemployed, provides support to church-based initiatives helping people who are unemployed.

Church Action with the Unemployed
45b Blythe Street
London E2 6LN
Tel. 071 729 9990

---

* Private trusts; see *A Guide to the Major Trusts; Vols 1 & 2*, published by The Directory for Social Change; also *Directory of Grant-Making Trusts*, published by the Charities Aid Foundation. All available through your library or volunteer bureau.
* TECs and LECs; may have access to funds for either training or enterprise projects.
* European Social Fund; local applications may be co-ordinated through the TEC/LEC, or Social Council if your area has one. Ask at the Citizens Advice Bureau.

Setting up an action group won't necessarily earn you money. However:

- It may lead to employment.
- Your time will be employed.
- You may have to work hard.
- You won't be made redundant.
- It will start to instil a sense of power and control both within you and your community.
- You may have the opportunity to use your existing skills, knowledge and experience.
- You will have an opportunity to learn new things.
- It will provide you with a new sense of structure in your life.
- It will provide you with a way in which to mix with more people.

In fact, starting an action group could provide you with all the elements of paid work plus additional benefits, along with the added bonus of self-fulfilment (lacking from so many jobs); and of course the pleasure you will get from making things happen.

The *Concise Oxford Dictionary* defines leisure as the 'Opportunity ... afforded by free time ....' Unfortunately when you are unemployed, with as much free time on your hands as you want, it becomes difficult to see it as leisure, and even more difficult to see any opportunities in it. The concept of leisure only seems valid when it is in contrast to other periods of time which are filled with activities ie work. For people in employment who have a large proportion of their waking time spoken for, leisure seems to have a very real and necessary place in life, to contrast with their work activities. There is a balance and certain amount of harmony in the two different aspects to their life.

Work provides an easy way in which to structure time; you could almost imagine Communists were referring to this and not religion as being the opiate of the people. It drugs the mind and keeps it contented by occupying it, saving it from the distress of having nothing to do. Minds, like our bodies, are made for activity. They become very upset when they are not given enough varied exercise. Work normally provides them with the necessary exercise and leisure provides the rest it needs to 'balance the books', or even provide an escape back to sanity after the stresses and strains of a demanding job. With work, leisure makes sense.

Difficulties arise when there is no longer a contrast possible. If you don't have a job, what place does leisure have? You don't feel the need to escape to the bliss of a night in front of the television any more. It loses its appeal after a while, and becomes simply another mind-deadening drug. The balance is upset, as the one contrasting activity of work is taken away. Now, all that seems to exist is a vast expanse of time, stretching into who knows where, dotted here and there with a few soaps on the TV to give some sense of continuity. Previously the leisure activities which only had a few hours dedicated to them, squeezed in between school work or job work, now sprawls out thinly over huge tracts of time, diluting the original pleasure you gained from them.

There is a need, then, to go back to the dictionary definition and remind ourselves that there are opportunities within the free time which is now available to you. Hopefully some of the previous chapters will already have provided you with some food for thought for developing your own ideas about possibilities. If you have decided to follow through some of your ideas, your time will already be looking rather different. If not, the task becomes how to transform the lack of routine which leads to boredom into something more positive.

Feelings of boredom can be terribly difficult to handle, and may lead on to more unpleasant feelings of either depression, or outbursts of aggression from frustration. Both are signs that the mind is shouting out for attention because boredom is dulling that fine thing which so badly needs constant change and stimulation. Since work is not presently available to provide that necessary stimulation and structure, a new alternative has to be found. Focusing on just job search activities is not enough for it, and the constant negative reinforcement from failed job applications can be positively damaging if there is nothing else to focus on or turn one's attention to afterwards.

So, if lack of money no longer permits the enjoyment of some of the activities which you may have enjoyed when in work, and the remaining ones just aren't enough, then new ways of providing your mind with change and stimulation must be found. Funnily enough, you may be feeling that you just want to get away from it all, which may have been the same feeling you had before, if you previously had a job. All that those feelings are saying is that you want to get away, not from your physical surroundings as such, but away from the discomfort you are feeling at not having enough things on your agenda which sufficiently interest you. Previously you may always have thought that if only you had the time you would get around to all those chores which have been waiting to be done for aeons. So why aren't you doing them now? The answer is because they are probably boring activities which you never wanted to do at the best of times, so you aren't likely to want to do them now. Forget about them for a while. Instead, let's have a look at some of the more interesting possibilities.

I must confess that even when I am in work, I can easily feel bored with my free time. The only time when I'm not is when I'm really looking forward to, or actually doing, something particularly interesting. It gives me something to focus on, out of the not very exciting here and now, which then becomes more bearable. It gives me a framework for the near future to help me keep it in perspective. But I'm lazy and frequently forget that I have to plan things ahead so that I *do* have things to look forward to. So when I'm feeling bored, I wake up to the fact that I need to get some more things underway, which then gets the enthusiasm going again. It's impossible for me to just get up and actually start an activity. Somehow that seems much too difficult, but setting a date in my diary for when I will do it is manageable. Phoning someone and making a commitment to go somewhere (perhaps just popping over for coffee) in the near future is much easier than putting on my coat to go now. And after filling up the diary with a few nice things to look forward to, the time is committed and spoken for (much the same as a day at work is). Planning in this way also helps me plan any expenditure I may incur, and allow me to save in good time.

Planning ahead can really help and may be the way in which you can start to enjoy your leisure time more, too. You might like to pin up a large calendar which shows the next few months at a glance; like the ones managers tend to have pinned on the walls behind their desks. They need them so they can schedule activities ahead of time, and also to serve as a reminder as to what's coming up next. Since you are going to become a manager — of your free time — then a calender will serve you well, too. You will be able to see where the yawning gaps are up ahead. You will be able to see at a glance, just why you feel such anxiety at the blankness of days — it's because there are so many of them, filled with the same few measly things to do. If you started to pencil in now the things you know you have to do in the future, you will probably be able to squeeze the year's activities into the space of a few days. In all those other, blank days lie the hidden opportunities.

Start off with some research. Have a look around at what activities and events are available locally. Your town hall's leisure and recreation department might have a diary of events for the forthcoming year. While you're at the town hall, call at the information desk where they may have other free brochures about forthcoming events organized by different independent groups. Scan noticeboards for fliers advertising activities which might be of interest and take down details. Think about where you might find other noticeboards, such as in the library, church hall, health centre, community hall, parks, galleries and museums. You may be able to think of more in your area. Find out where the best boards are and resolve to check them out regularly, to help you plan ahead. You may have a free local paper. These are often good places to find notices about forthcoming markets, fairs, jumble sales, lectures etc. Make sure you keep your eye on the 'What's On' section.

It may be that in the past it has been too easy to take your area and what it has to offer for granted. Once you start looking you may well be surprised to find out what is available and how much of it is free or offers concessionary rates. If you think not enough concessionary rates are available, or that they are not reasonable enough, you could tackle the issue by forming a local action group (see previous chapter). Charging £5 entrance fee might seem reasonable to someone who is in paid employment but who has a simple lack of understanding about how prohibitive the price still is if you are on benefits.

Your area may have a number of the following available:

Cultural Activities

Plays put on by local drama groups; displays of arts and crafts by students at local colleges or who have been attending evening classes; special exhibitions at art galleries and museums — they may also have lectures, guest speakers and demonstrations.

Regular Events

Most areas have some sort of special yearly event. I'm thinking of country fairs, carnivals, festivals, May Day celebrations, even bonfire night celebrations. Chat to people about which regular events they can remember throughout the year. If some of them have costly entrance fees, you could start planning in advance to try to obtain special discount rates for concessions and for block bookings for your community.

Places of Interest

Although the more famous venues can have pricey admission rates, there are many others which are free or which offer concessionary rates. You might like to do some research first at your library to find out more about local history. If there is a museum you might also find some interesting starting points there, and discover where the remains of an ancient fort, castle or barrow can be found. You may also be able to visit places where famous people used to live, and become inspired to take up a line of research to find out more about their lives. You could start compiling the information you are gleaning and use it to write a leaflet or book on your findings, or draw up a local guide. Could this launch you into a new enterprise?

Walking Tours

Although common in London, which has a rich source of material for tours, they may not be so well established in your area. See if your library has any leaflets, or even books available on interesting walks. If not, you could devise some yourself based on nature trails, lives of famous people, historical trails, trails for children, trails suitable for people with disabilities, or whatever else your locality has to offer, and turn this pursuit into a new enterprise, too. Your local Tourist Board may have funds available to help you get started.

Sporting Events

Have a look through your local paper's sports pages to check on forthcoming events. If you've never been to an ice-hockey game, why not take the chance to go now. If you've never seen a basketball match, give it a try. There's even a local conker competition where my sister lives — and it's great fun! So before you dismiss opportunities out of hand, take advantage of the time you have to investigate as many different events as you can; you may get a job tomorrow and not have a chance like this again. Also, every time you go out into new situations you increase your chance of hearing about vacancies as they arise, or spotting opportunities for a new business venture. It may also provide you with some ideas to take back to your more immediate neighbourhood. For example, if you see how well the local tug-of-war competition went down, you might see a possibility for setting one up in your area, too.

Social Groups

There may be a number of social groups which you could join and which have the benefit of organizing events for you. For example, there may be clubs linked with your place of worship; one for people who are unemployed; one for single parents; linked to a political party; etc. And again, if they don't offer reasonable concessionary rates, campaign for them to be improved, or for staggered payment facilities to be introduced. If you can show they could increase their membership significantly by doing so, they will probably take your suggestions more seriously.

Cultural or Religious Centre

There may be lots of activities based around your local place of worship. Special performances by choirs or musicians; talks; fêtes; special celebrations. Ask what is available where you live. You might also like to take the opportunity to get to know about other religions and cultures. Developing an understanding of different groups of people can greatly benefit us not only on a personal level but also on a wider community level, too.

Whatever you see advertised which interests you, mark the date down on your wallchart calendar. Soon you'll start to see those gaps disappearing beneath reminders of lectures, plays, jumble sales, church fêtes, planned walks and attending meetings with your new social groups.

• BUT THERE'S REALLY NOTHING AVAILABLE

Perhaps what you might mean is that there is nothing available which interests you, or which you can afford. Fair enough. You may live in a twee area with lots of amateur operatics, but with little provision for small children. Lucky you. This presents an excellent opportunity to organize things yourself, or at least get others together who have similar interests. Some events can be just for fun, while others may turn into money-generating projects which in turn can help fund other community initiatives. It may also give you some ideas for a mini-enterprise or lead to the generation of other self-employment initiatives. Getting an action group going has already been covered in the previous chapter, which stressed the need to follow your enthusiasms. The same applies here. Decide what you (on your own, or as a group) would like to see established. It may be a single major event, such as a festival to encourage local talent, or a special sports event. Or it may be a whole calendar of events planned throughout the year which will serve either a specific group of people, or the area as a whole. Here are some suggestions to serve as a springboard for your own ideas:

- Barbecue
- Street carnival, or one held on a local green space, in a hall, or other venue
- Pantomime
- Concert — pop, rock, classical, cabaret, music hall, old-time, sixties
- Treasure hunt
- Play
- Dance — ballroom, rock and roll, disco, or an exhibition of special dance (eg Indian, Irish, clog, ballet)
- Football, tennis, bowls, badminton, swimming, table tennis tournament; in fact any sport you choose
- Car boot sale
- Bring and buy sale
- Singing or other talent competition
- Jumble sale
- Sponsored event, like a distance walk, run, jog, swim
- Fun events, like a pancake race on Shrove Tuesday. For continuity, each year the champion defends their title (even my sister had to defend her conker championship!)
- Historical event simulation — such as a famous battle
- Re-instatement of a traditional event
- Tie-ins with a local radio station
- Introduce a particular culture's day of celebration to the wider community.

Although community events are important, you won't be wanting to spend all your time either out of the house or with groups of people. It is a question of balance. You may already have an on-going interest or hobby which takes up part of your time, but this may no longer be enough on its own, or it may be that you have never had the time before to think seriously about following any particular pursuits. A good browse through your library may give you some ideas. Scan the shelves which you wouldn't normally, or which seem less obviously connected with hobbies. For example, the natural history section may give you some ideas around fossils, shells, mushrooms, herbs, trees or plants; biography might arouse your interest in a famous person who has always secretly fascinated you (could you start an interest society based around their life and works?). The children's library might also provide clues. In the meantime, consider some of the following:

Collecting

Whatever intrigues and delights you, can form the basis of a collection. Obviously you will want to concentrate on things which can be collected for free, or almost free. Pebbles, old keys, packaging designs, nature's cast-offs, birthday or Christmas cards, fabrics, buttons, bookmarks, old tools. Whatever you like and gives you pleasure, and in which you can see beauty is a possibility. When you have a small collection together you can consider how to display or make other use of it. For example, the pebbles you have collected could become painted doorstops or paper-weights; you could learn how to frame, so that you could display the cards you have collected, or use them for decoupage, cutting up the cards and sticking them down on card or paper to create a decorative picture; the buttons could turn into a valuable collection which you could sell on. Each collection could have the makings of an enterprise within it, but even so, do it initially because you love the objects you're collecting.

Crafts

You could advertise or ask around for someone to teach you a craft or other skill which will allow you to pursue another hobby. For example, there may be a skilled wood carver, carpenter, gardener or herbalist living nearby. Ask around.

Board Games

Board games are often thought of as just children's games, but I know few adults who don't get excited when they're winning at Monopoly, and just remember how Trivial Pursuits took the world by storm. Dust off the board games in your house, including puzzles. You could establish a games group which holds regular sessions or one which offers a swap shop. You could even club together to buy new games, too; or what about developing your own board game? I'm sure the people who designed Trivial Pursuits never looked back, and neither did Alfred Mosher Butts who invented Scrabble when he could find little work as an architect during the Depression. I'm sure he never regretted the opportunities which lack of work presented to him.

Gardening

Investigate the possibility of allotments. Not only is it therapeutic to grow things, it could also provide you with food at little cost, and might even produce an excess to sell on.

Meditating

It is easy to forget that although you may not presently be working you still need to unwind from the different sorts of stresses in your life. Learning how to meditate can be a real challenge, and bring true benefits. Although there may be groups which you could join in order to learn, it is just as easy to learn the basic principles from a good book in your library, such as *Meditation*, James Hewitt (Teach Yourself Books 1978).

Learn Something New

Now might be a good time to realize a latent interest or even discover a hidden talent. Consider some of the more unusual possibilities like learning how to read tarot cards, or people's palms or tea leaves. Again you might be surprised at the potential for self-employment which arises out of what starts as a casual hobby or pastime.

Personal Research

This may appeal to the more bookish, such as myself. I am the sort of person who loves delving into research and following my enthusiasms wherever they lead. At the moment it is trees, and one tree in particular which I can't find in any of the books. I'd like to find out not only what it is, but also its other properties which draw me to it on a deeper, spiritual level. There are also more practical research projects, like family histories. This can become a totally absorbing hobby, leading to all sorts of fascinating discoveries. I can remember a colleague once telling me that he and his partner had both gone back through their family histories only to discover that although they each came from different parts of the country, their ancestors had already crossed paths before them. Another friend has discovered she is related to Roget who developed the famous thesaurus. But anything which arouses your interest can form the basis for a research project, which in turn could lead to all sorts of different possibilities, not least of which is getting your findings published.

Talk to other people about what interests they have. Through their enthusiasm they might spark off your own, enough to make you want to join in with them and perhaps form an interest group or club. And again, it may develop into something more serious and lead you into discovering its business potential.

• TREATS

Despite the planned events there may well be times when the clock seems to stop, and the world seems to pause between seconds. The next event isn't for a while, and quite frankly you feel a bit down. This is the time when you need a treat. We all need treats every now and again to keep our spirits up. The difficulty is that we are now conditioned to think only in terms of expensive luxuries. There are alternatives; it's just that we've forgotten them, encouraged by the media's false images of a materialistic Nirvana. Spend some time thinking about all the possible ways in which you could treat yourself — or others (paradoxically, giving can be more therapeutic and cheering than receiving). You could turn it into a family or group challenge, to draw up a list of as many treats as possible. Here are some ideas:

- Freshly baked bread
- A flower
- A long bath with as many trimmings as possible, perhaps even by candle-light
- A properly laid table, even though it's only egg and chips (*a la carte*)
- An afternoon away from everyone
- A walk to a favourite place
- A big breakfast with as many trimmings as possible
- Playing old records
- The smell of cut grass
- A hug
- An afternoon cup of tea in a cafe after a long walk
- Growing something from seed.

Special treats for kids could be something as simple as arranging a stop-over with a friend; learning a magic or card trick to show them; taking them for a mystery tour; making a walk turn into a nature experience based on insects, trees, clouds or birds.

You could have fun coming up with different ideas, which may be a god-send when you most need it. You could think about consolidating your ideas and producing a marketable leaflet, brochure or book.

• HOLIDAYS

While on benefit you are allowed to have two weeks' holiday, so long as you leave an address where you can be contacted should a job come up. Ask for a Holiday Form when you sign on.

Although a world cruise might not be on the agenda, holidays may still be possible. You could borrow camping equipment and spend a week or two in the wild, under canvas. If you walk to your destination the costs should be absolutely minimal — and my friends assure me camping really can be a lot of fun. Youth hostels are a bit more expensive but still remarkably good value, and not just for school children. You could even enquire beforehand as to whether you could help out as assistant warden or, if you have a suitable qualification, as a sports leader.

Winged Fellowship Trust
Angel House
20–32 Pentonville Road
London N1 9XD
Tel. 071 833 2594

Mencap Holiday Office
119 Drake Street
Rochdale
Lancs OL16 1PZ
Tel. 0706 54111

There are volunteer holidays, for example accompanying people with physical or learning disabilities: contact the Winged Fellowship Trust or Mencap, or call in to your local volunteer bureau. See also *Working Holidays* published by the Central Bureau for Educational Visits and Exchanges, and also *Home from Home* which is about exchanging your home for someone else's for a holiday break. There is also the Working

Weekends on Organic Farms (WWOOF) scheme where, in exchange for working on an organic farm, you receive free board and lodging and transport to and from the local station. The scheme also operates abroad.

Working Weekends on Organic Farms
19 Bradford Road
Lewes
Sussex BN7 1RB
Send an SAE for further information.

Your local church or religious centre may also have details of retreats which may be available to you. I often need to go on mini-retreats which might only last for a few hours in the afternoon or morning, but they give me valuable solo-time. I go to my favourite park and sit in my favourite spot, and just bliss out for a while. Sometimes it's to turn over a problem, other times it's just to get away from distractions and to find a space in which to be quiet. You might like to plan your own mini-retreats, too.

Leisure is easy when you have a job. It becomes the desirable commodity which you acquire in exchange for forfeiting the rest of your time in work. That can be a very high price to pay. Fortunately you are in a position now, however temporary or long-term, to find those opportunities which the dictionary definition of leisure alludes to. It may initially mean a bit more hard work to knock your time into shape and to find the right balance and mix of different activities. You may want to enlist the help and support from others, but however you do it, follow your enthusiasms, go where your excitements take you, and who knows it may even lead you to that long-forgotten dream: employment.

One of the most difficult feelings to handle which being unemployed produces is that of powerlessness. Not only is the task of finding a job difficult, but also with little or no spare cash to hand, you can feel another sort of powerlessness. Activities become severely restricted; costly repairs either go unattended or create debt; saving money is an almost laughable idea; every single penny is accounted for in every single week. This inevitably creates the feeling of lack of freedom. Money isn't everything, but we still need it.

It may be helpful to mention here the New Age concept of abundance. I feel sure that most of us would jump at the chance if we were offered a life of abundance. Being unemployed, the likelihood of that happening can seem totally unlikely, and yet abundance has nothing to do with how much money you do or don't have. Think about how many rich but miserable people there are. Money cannot create a feeling of abundance in those people whose spirit is lacking in feelings of abundance. Unfortunately, when you are unemployed it is the spirit which goes out of some people; it feels like their life has drained out of them; they feel a sense of poverty; they feel they are worth nothing because they no longer have a job. It is easy to see then why being unemployed makes you less likely to feel abundant. An impoverished spirit leads to a feeling of living an impoverished life. But if abundance has nothing to do with money and everything to do with feelings within, then it is possible for change to take place. One can move from a feeling of poverty to one of abundance regardless of the actual money you have in your pocket. And when one has identified one's true path in life, and starts to move in line with it, blockages clear away and one's needs become more easily met — the definition of abundance. I'm only too well aware of this happening in my own life. From living a life out of keeping with my true self and being constantly in debt, I am now moving closer to my real life aim and finding that although not rich by any stretch of the imagination, my needs are all being met and I no longer have debts. Chapter 6 explains about this in more detail.

In learning to find out about our true selves, learning about what our inner needs are, and understanding that when we make an inner shift, our outer reality changes too (things work out more easily, we suddenly find that we are getting what we need etc.), we allow a big shift to take place in feelings of powerlessness. Suddenly we realize we can do something about our situation, not by relying on Employers, The System, The Government or any of those Others, but by relying on ourselves. We change, and things change around us. Perhaps this is the most basic element to self-sufficiency: learning that we can affect what happens to us, and that we do indeed have power. To help us 'read' the messages which surround us and which are there to signpost the way, we have what some people call our intuition to trust. If you feel that yours is under-developed, you could try to find ways in which to exercise it and bring it more into being so that you become more able to rely on your self for finding the right way forward.

As soon as you start to make moves towards that inner transformation, changes will start to take place, but in the meantime it may be useful to look at the more practical ways in which to regain that all-important sense of control over your life. As was mentioned, the restrictions imposed by a lack of spare cash can be very difficult to cope with, so making the money which you do have go further can only help. Adopting as many self-sufficient and shared-sufficiency measures as you can will facilitate not only that, but also encourage a greater sense of independence and pride in its own right. And if you have children, you can share your valuable learning with them so that they grow up with the advantage of knowing how to be as self-sufficient as possible.

If you have read Chapter 2 you may have analysed your outgoings already and trimmed back as much as you can. It is also useful to analyse your needs. Go beyond what it is you want (eg a car — or to keep the one you have) and identify what actually creates the need. A straightforward answer might be that you need a car because of the poor public transport service where you live. At first sight this may seem a water-tight reason for keeping your own wheels, but have a look at the other options which might meet your needs besides the costly one of running a car. One of those options might be to campaign locally for an improvement in transport services. If there is no joy there, you could form an action group (see Chapter 10) to raise funds to buy a community bus, van or car. Establishing a car-share scheme might be another option. Whenever a need arises, going through the process of identifying what is behind the need and then looking at other options to satisfy that need may prove enlightening — and may help you come up with some cost-saving options. But with any measure you consider, it's important to try to do it out of a sense of joy rather than begrudging every economy; otherwise it will be only too easy to feel even more impoverished. If it seems like a particularly difficult change to make, I find it helps if I focus on what I intend to do with the money saved. In this way you're not saving just for money's sake, but for a more concrete reason instead, like a new pair of shoes or a weekend break. Decide what you will do with any money saved and stay focused on that. If you have children it will help if they know what the economies are going towards as well.

But this is beginning to sound as though adopting more self-sufficient measures means nothing more than looking at what you can sacrifice. You may be pleasantly surprised to find that the opposite is true as you begin to discover new pleasures and rediscover old ones. Remember that the more you have to buy, the less self-reliant you can be and the more difficulties it can create. So with this in mind, let's have a look at some ways in which you can cut down on the amount you have to spend.

· WHERE YOU LIVE

Although you may be getting Housing Benefit to help pay for the roof over your head, actually keeping a home running can be very costly, especially with heating and cooking overheads. In particular, heating can be very expensive, but made even more so if you live in a poorly insulated building. While you are on benefit you may be eligible for insulation grants through your local council. Enquire at the town hall. Improving insulation will help enormously and even if you are not eligible for a grant, there are some simple draught-proofing measures you can take. For example, folding lengths of paper about three or four centimetres wide (one and a half inches) into V-shapes and pushing them around loose-fitting windows has helped improve insulation in my home enormously over the cold winter months. You can also make attractive draught excluders for the bottom of doors from old clothes and scraps of material sewn into tube shapes and stuffed with old pairs of tights or any other fabric oddments. Curtains hung on brass rails over doors help keep the wind from whistling around on wintery nights.

The humble newspaper comes into its own in helping with insulation problems, too. Placed underneath carpets it helps cut down on draughts through floorboards, and made into a pâpier-mâché it can be used to fill gaps around skirting boards. But on a grander scale you could raise the issue of neighbourhood use of energy, contacting Neighbourhood Energy Action and perhaps forming your own group to look into establishing local energy-producing schemes. You may also wish to campaign for more large-scale insulation improvements to be made to council housing stock, or find ways in which the community at large can take action, perhaps through the formation of a community business to carry out the work.

Depending on your circumstances you could consider more radical measures to finding ways of living in cheaper, or better housing. There are a handful of groups which have formed around the country to find their own answer. They are now in the process of building their own homes and communities. This is no small undertaking, but if you feel this may be your ideal solution contact the Neighbourhood Initiatives Foundation (see Chapter 10, page 117). Or, at the other extreme, you could think of simply selling up and taking to the road in a camper van, or even the high seas as one couple did. But if you have a home and the rent or mortgage is being paid, it might make more sense simply to find ways in which to make it run as economically as possible. You might even like to start looking at providing your own entertainment to cut down on television and video viewing. Playing games with the kids instead of letting them lounge in front of the box not only saves money on electricity but is more fun for family life. And instead of thinking that your only personal options lie between channels one and four, or the pub which you can't really afford, plan some alternative entertainments with your partner or friends. It needn't cost anything if you use what you already have available (pack of cards; board games; your imagination). You could cut down on electricity bills — and you might just have some fun. We tend to think of entertainment as something which happens to us, forgetting that we can just as easily, and perhaps more enjoyably, make our own.

Neighbourhood Energy Action
26 Bedford Square
London WC1
Tel. 071 636 4066

▪ FOOD

A household's major weekly expenditure goes on food, and since it is a basic necessity there would seem to be little one could do in terms of cutting back. However, there are ways in which the food you do buy in can be supplemented by other produce to help save the odd pound here and there.

We forget that in its natural state all food is provided free by nature. Our remote ancestors weren't exactly au fait with taking a trolley to do their weekly stocking up! Instead they lived off the riches of the land, and eventually learned ways in which to preserve foods which were plentiful in season so that they could be enjoyed at a later date. This, you could say, heralded the beginning of convenience foods. Now the majority of us automatically buy a great many things ready prepared for us to pop into the oven or microwave, from simple vegetables to whole meals. This fantastic growth in convenience foods has found its market in the needs of people whose time is short, especially those who not only have paid employment but also have to run a home and family as well. One of the advantages of being without work is that with the extra time available there's an opportunity to break out of the habit of buying those costly ready-prepared foods. It might also be a good time to consider cutting back on meat, which is extremely expensive compared to other protein sources such as beans. Do some research to find some recipes which don't use meat and if your family would shriek at the very word 'vegetarian', still serve meat dishes but only once or twice a week instead.

Make Your Own

There are few better things than the smell of freshly baked bread, pies or cakes. You could do some costings and work out if it would be cheaper for you to make your own instead of sticking to only shop-bought produce. With a local bulk-buy food co-op established you could cut costs even more (see page 112). You could also think of selling on or bartering any surplus foods you make, to help cover production costs and to go towards other items you buy in.

Fresh vegetables tend to be cheaper when they are in season. Take advantage of this and buy accordingly. You might also like to think of finding ways to preserve those in-season fruits and vegetables, perhaps through freezing, making jams, chutneys or purées, making up dishes which use them and freezing them, pickling, drying etc. In this way you can make best use of cheap produce and be self-sufficient in them when others are having to pay premium prices.

If you like the odd tipple you might also like to take the opportunity to learn how to make your own. You can either buy kits which have everything you need, plus the instructions, or you could do some research into making your own wines and beers, like plum, dandelion or elderflower (which makes a delicious champagne-like wine). Making your own is a lot cheaper than buying, and perhaps more satisfying knowing you have made it yourself. Invite some friends around to sample the fruits of your labour, and even trade a bottle or two in exchange for things you need.

You could also investigate the wider potential in foods. For example, from the humble soya bean you can make your own milk substitute, tofu and tempeh (meat alternatives) and with the remnants you are left with a soup base, shampoo, washing up liquid and even furniture polish, not to mention the bran to use as an addition to either soups or breakfast cereals. The soya bean must be the ultimate self-sufficiency product.

Have a look as well into making your own soft cheeses and yoghurts, which could cost you a fraction of the shop-bought versions.

Grow Your Own

You would need a fair-sized plot of land in order to grow enough food to be totally self-sufficient but there is still the opportunity to augment your intake of food with produce which you grow yourself. You might be lucky enough to have a large garden which you could turn over either wholly or partly to 'grow your own'. And remember that some flowers can also be eaten, such as nasturtiums, carnations, roses, marigolds and elderflowers. If you don't have a garden, ask around to see if there is someone who would like to trade the use of theirs in exchange for some of what you produce.

Allotments are another possibility. Contact your local town hall to see if there are any available or whether there is a waiting list you could join. Also ask friends if they know of others available, too. If not, there may be a plot of local waste land which you might identify as being ideal for allotments and which could be converted. See if you can form an action group to get things moving (see Chapter 10).

But even if you have little more than a back yard, a balcony or window-sill, there are still things you can grow yourself. A recent gardening programme showed that potatoes can be grown very successfully in large plant-pots, so why not give a few other vegetables a try? If you're not too green-fingered ask for help from someone who is, perhaps at a local garden centre or shop.

We eat many foods which either contain seeds or are seeds, such as tomatoes, beans, peas, apples and other fruits. Root vegetables like carrots and potatoes easily sprout if left in a warm dark place for a while. I remember growing many a carrot top in a saucer of water when I was young. So do some research and start to see each food you bring into the house in terms of whether you can grow on from what you have bought.

If you are considering starting to eat more vegetables, herbs can be invaluable in transforming even the humble potato into some exotic dish. Herbs can be expensive to buy yet are very easy to grow in plant pots and window boxes. Try your hand at parsley, basil, chives or coriander. Even though you may have to buy seeds to start you off, you could share the cost of packets with a neighbour, and once they are established the perennial plants should go on indefinitely.

Along the same lines you could have fresh salad or stir-fry ingredients the year round by sprouting seeds and beans. Beansprouts are perhaps the ones most people know and are a main ingredient in Chinese dishes. They are deliciously crunchy and fresh and like all sprouts are incredibly nutritious — but they can be expensive to buy. However, you can sprout your own from mung beans which are available from health food shops. Simply soak the beans overnight, strain and put them in a glass jar with some muslin over the top. Keep them out of daylight and rinse the seeds daily until they have sprouted. The same goes for any bean or seed, although small seeds like alfalfa can be grown on damp tissue paper in the same way as mustard cress.

Pick Your Own

Nature provides us with her bounty, and in the open wild it is there for the picking — so long as you treat her with respect and pick carefully rather than plundering without thought. Most people tend to think only in terms of blackberries or mushrooms from the wild, but there are many other foods available: nuts, edible flowers, fruits, berries, green vegetables, herbs, spices, seaweeds and shellfish. That's quite a list, and obviously if you live near the sea-shore you can take full advantage of what's on offer. If you feel lacking in confidence about what is and isn't safe to eat, do some research at your local library. A good book to start you off is *Food for Free* by Richard Mabey.

▪ RECYCLING

Our awareness has been greatly increased over the last few years about the need to recycle refuse, and collection bins for bottles, tins and papers are now common sights. However, there may be ways in which you could recycle in your own home and to your direct benefit.

Clothes are an obvious item which lends itself to this. Children's clothes are passed down from one child to the next while adult clothes are recycled through jumble sales or charity shops. Now might be a good opportunity to learn how to make even greater use of last year's cast-offs, perhaps by learning how to restyle and make your own patterns at a dressmaking class. Total discards could still be made use of by using the fabric to make draught excluders, patchwork quilts, rag rugs, patchwork curtains for doorways, cushions, covers for books and soft toys. You could also put old jumpers to use by re-knitting them up as throw-overs, shawls and woolly socks for chilly winter evenings when you're sitting around indoors. You could even find yourself launched into forming the basis for a new mini-enterprise, which really makes your recycled material pay its way.

We all now handle masses of paper in different forms, most of which is either thrown away or sent to the recycling bin. You could put some of it to use as pâpier-mâché to make crafted items and for DIY purposes (see above, page 138). You could also pulp it to make your own hand-crafted paper — the ultimate in recycling. Receiving post in envelopes which have been recycled with a sticky label is now commonly accepted so make your own glue paste and use scraps of paper cut into label size. And all that junk mail you receive could be benefiting you since the letters are normally printed on high quality paper which commands a top price when sold for recycling in bulk. Relieve your neighbourhood of its junk mail, find somewhere to store it and sell it on to your (or the community's) profit.

Make it a fun project with family and friends to consider as many alternative uses for each item you normally throw away. Even egg shells can be used as biodegradable growing pots for seedlings, as can empty toilet paper rolls. Once you start to look at the potential in objects, your mind opens to lots of alternatives which can either benefit you directly or which can be sold on or form part of an exchange. And for those items you really can't wait to see the back of, there is always the car boot sale (you don't need a car to hire a pitch), or you may be able to arrange a swap with someone.

• CREATE YOUR OWN PRODUCTS

With so many training courses and 'how to' books available, and so much expertise going to waste, it should be relatively easy to pick up a few basic skills to learn how to make a number of items for yourself instead of having to rely on expensive shop-bought products. Clothes and food have already been mentioned, but you could also learn how to make your own simple furniture, soft furnishings, cosmetics, toiletries, toys and gifts. Just think what enjoyment you could get from developing and using your own range of products, and what an even bigger thrill if you can find a buyer for any surplus you might have. Could this also form the basis for a self-employment venture?

▪ REPAIRS

Everything seems to be ticking over well, and then the washing machine decides to dump its load all over the kitchen floor. Unless you are a member of a LETS scheme (see page 114) you are then at the mercy of what seems like the exorbitant fees which plumbers charge. How much better if you could rely on your own skills to repair the fault. With the time you now have available, you could take the opportunity to learn how to do a wide range of household repair jobs. Again, see what classes are available locally, what expertise you could tap into or local skills-swap scheme you could join (see page 49), and even what books are available. There are a whole range of basic repairs you could learn to do safely: plumbing, electrical, mechanical, furniture, ceramics, shoes, clothes. Have a look around to see what opportunities are available. Again, this might prove to be the basis for a sound business venture, perhaps organized at the community level.

▪ LOOK AFTER YOUR OWN HEALTH

Despite the health service, being ill is becoming more expensive. You may be eligible for concessions if you are on benefit, but how much better not to have to have any dental treatment in the first place, not to have to wear glasses anyway, and not to need any vital prescriptions. By looking after your health you can avoid having to be reliant on many things. You may also be able to do things like improve your eyesight or at least prevent it from deteriorating any more by learning and practising the Bates Eye Method. Find a copy of *Good Sight Without Glasses* by Dr Bates at your local library, or ask them to order a copy for you.

There are also many simple techniques taken from complementary therapies which you can learn and which may bring relief from the more simple complaints. For example, pressure-point massage, which you can do by yourself, stimulates the blocked energy in your body which is at the root of many problems. Headaches, stress, simple back ache may all be relieved in this way rather than having to rely on expensive pain-relieving pills.

You could also learn how to use plants such as herbs and flowers, or even simple food substances like honey or vinegar, to make home-made remedies in the form of ointments, creams, poultices, and syrups. However, it is important that you learn how to do this properly because herbs, for example, are drugs, and they can be dangerous if not used properly.

Do some research at your local library, health food shop or alternative health centre to find out about the different therapies or home remedies which you could learn and put to use. Evening classes may be available in some subjects. If you become really interested you may find yourself looking towards a future career in this growing field.

See Chapter 14 for more detail on staying physically fit and on proper relaxation as a way of maintaining good health.

• TRANSPORT

The most self-reliant form of transport is provided by moving under your own steam. Learn to make use of that resource as much as possible since it is free, hardly ever lets you down, and is the perfect exercise. But for longer distances, think about forming a local transport action group (see page 110). You could improve transport facilities by creating a pool of car and bike users who would be willing to share, as well as by taking action to buy your own community transport.

• YOUR INVESTMENTS

Investments? Me? Yes, you may not have any stocks and shares but you may have a few items which you have invested in and which could now be helping you become more self-reliant. Turf out the cupboards and the garage and see what treasures you have stored up: garden tools, DIY tools, camera, bicycle, sewing machine, food processor, car, bike, space (disused garage, spare room, attic), typewriter, computer, garden, greenhouse, knowledge, expertise etc. Have a good stocktake and make a list of all those items which could be put to better use, either on a community level, in terms of making your life better by saving you money, or by creating the means through which to earn an income.

Feeling that you are on your own in trying to deal with unemployment and that you are somehow separate and cut off from the rest of the world can make life feel very hard to endure. But it is true that a problem shared makes the problem seem more manageable, so although being as self-sufficient as possible may help the money go further, *shared-sufficiency* can help the good feelings go further, too. Friends of the Earth (see page 102) produce a whole range of useful publications on ways to put this into practice. Talk to others about your ideas and see whether together you can find ways in which to solve common problems.

13 ▪ *Looking After Your Mind*

The psychological effects of both becoming and being unemployed can be devastating. Money can be a problem but at least it is tangible and efforts can be made to sort it out; but difficult emotions are more ephemeral and less easily held up to the light to even see how they could possibly be dealt with. If left unresolved though, they can prevent any real progress being made, may even interfere with opportunities and jeopardize any chances when they do appear. Ultimately they can become destructive. It is important therefore to pay attention to your feelings and address any difficulties. Being unemployed creates its own stresses and strains and so it is important to keep yourself in the fittest mental as well as physical state in order to ensure that you are best able to cope with life's new demands, one of which may be the prospect of another six months without work.

Since we are all individuals we react in our own personal way to finding ourselves unemployed. Some people may feel thoroughly relieved to be leaving behind the responsibilities of a particular job, while it is more common for rather more negative emotions to be felt. Initially some may be felt very keenly such as shock and disbelief at being made redundant. These feelings are easy to identify and seem very clear cut, but as time progresses they can become less easily identifiable as they swirl around in a confusion of depressing thoughts. If the possibility of redundancy has been there for a long time, those initial feelings may have worn away by the time the actual day arrives, but other feelings may be lurking in wait, ready for the first opportunity to strike.

Chapter 6 talks about loss of identity and self-worth in more detail, so do read it if you haven't done so already. It's important that you start to discover genuine feelings of self-esteem; ones which don't rely on the vagaries of the job market — or any other outer or material thing. Genuine feelings of self-worth are abiding, are not dependent on The Boss's whims and can survive even major upsets such as redundancy and unemployment.

Restoring a pattern and aim in life is important. Without a sense of structure, boredom can so easily sneak into your life in the invidious way it does. I hope the previous chapters will have given you some ideas to start you off thinking about the whole range of opportunities which lie in wait for you. It may have been difficult to notice them through that cloud of pent-up emotions, but once the way is clear it's possible to see ways in which to transform the experience of unemployment from the negative to the positive. You can start to see how you might be able to make it work for you, not against you.

As mentioned earlier, you can start by removing the uncertainty about your future. Accept that you may well be out of work for the next three or six months. It could be that you're actually offered a job tomorrow, in which case great! But if you're not, it helps to have a sense of how much time you have to play around with. Knowing you have six months ahead of you turns the yawning chasm of future time into something much more manageable and for which you can plan. You are giving yourself more certainty.

Once you have a time-scale to provide the basic framework you can then start to structure the time within it. Chapter 11 describes the use of a wallchart to help build up a visual picture of what lies ahead. And if the answer is nothing more than the days you sign on and the odd birthday or two, then it becomes only too clear that there is a lot of scope for you to build other things into your life. You have the opportunity now to weave as appealing, creative and satisfying a pattern as you like. A day on job-search activities, a day researching a business idea, meetings with the credit union community

action group, volunteer work, classes for enjoyment or
learning new skills, courses, interest groups . . . . The scope is
vast; it is also a challenge. But without clearing the way
through those difficult and blocking emotions, it may seem
like the challenge is overwhelming and one which makes you
turn away, perhaps to the comfort of apathy instead. It is so
important therefore to find a way of airing those unresolved
issues, and untangle that uncomfortable mass of emotions,
thoughts and feelings.

▪ GETTING HELP

You may feel that enough face has already been lost just
through not having a job, that the prospect of letting even
close family members or friends see how upset and vulnerable
you are feeling may be too uncomfortable to consider. If this
is the case consider making use of available counselling
services in your area. There may be a 'drop-in' centre for
people who are unemployed, or a special counselling service.
Your previous employer may have made provision for
counselling support if you have been part of a major
redundancy exercise. Memberships of professional
organizations also sometimes offer redundancy counselling;
check it out. If you are unsure about what sort of provision
is available in your area, ask at your local Citizens Advice
Bureau. If there is absolutely no provision whatsoever, you
could consider channelling your energies into getting
something started (see Chapter 10). Read *Self-Help Groups:
Getting started – keeping going* by Judy Wilson. Get a copy from
your library, or ask them to order a copy for you.

Local community or religious leaders may also be another
source of information or help. They may know of ad hoc
groups of people who are in the same situation and who
regularly get together. They may also be able to recommend
someone who is either a trained or untrained counsellor;
someone who may have gone through a similar experience to

your own. You could also ask your doctor for information about local groups including MIND, whose local branch may be running special self-help groups.

MIND
National Association for Mental Health
22 Harley Street
London W1N 2ED
Tel. 071 637 0741

Here are some other places which might have useful information:

- Volunteer bureau
- Information department at your town hall
- Library
- Local newspapers
- Community centres
- Noticeboards.

With the loss of a job, colleagues and friends sometimes go too. This can make it seem like a double blow because now your social support is also diminished. And although family members might be supportive initially, they too may start to feel that they can't cope entirely alone with the emotional 'dumping' process you need to undergo. Besides finding additional support through counselling, it may help to start forming new social contacts by joining in a number of different activities (see Chapter 9).

In whichever way you choose to tackle the problem of sorting out the confusion in your head, it's important that you do so. To seek counselling help and support doesn't mean you are mad, weak, pathetic, less of a man or woman or any of the other connotations you think it might have. What it does mean is that you are human just like everyone else; that you are brave in being prepared to confront difficult issues; that you are making the best positive move possible; that you are moving towards clearing the way so that you can start moving forward more easily through this new and potentially exciting phase in your life; that you are preparing yourself to open up to new opportunities as they present themselves to you. You have nothing to lose, but plenty to gain. Go forward.

Having a job can be a very unhealthy occupation. Because much of your time is spoken for, little is left over to concentrate on your poor body which is put through its daily rigours — a mixture of slouching at desks or in cars and dashing hastily from one appointment/meeting/chore to the next. Hastily grabbed meals on the run, topped up with lashings of stress and strain, washed down with the long, slow commuting nightmare home — the regular daily diet. No wonder people feel exhausted at the end of a day's work. Unfortunately, out of a desperate need to relax, things are made worse with a few pints or gin and tonics too many, and take-away dinners come into their own because you're too exhausted to be bothered about cooking. I've been there; you may have, too.

With unemployment at least you've escaped the madness of that merry-go-round, even though it might be only temporarily. Unfortunately, there are different stresses, strains and worries to replace the old ones and these too can also affect your health just as easily. In fact the one thing you probably now feel you have plenty of is worry, worry, worry. This is understandable, and I hope the last chapter will have raised your awareness of how to cope with the pressures and difficulties you will inevitably be facing. The mind and body are inextricably linked, so whatever goes on in your mind will be echoed through your body in one way or another. Even suppressed emotions which you think are well under control will eventually find an outlet. They're like little children who constantly need attention, to be noticed: 'Here I am. Look at me!' they cry. If you don't pay them the attention they need, they will continue crying out until you *have* to notice them in the form of a cold, a headache or a sore back. You may have been tempted to skip the last chapter on emotions, thinking you have them well under control, but thought you wanted to read this one because you could do with a bit more energy, or feel more like one hundred per cent. Yet if there are pent-up emotions, or issues which need dealing with and which you are trying to ignore, you may find it incredibly difficult, if not impossible, to make any headway with your health at all.

Having said that, the mind/body link works both ways. For example, if I am feeling a bit under the weather for no apparent reason, a good course of vitamin C normally helps to put things to rights and if I haven't been eating properly, it quickly shows in how well I feel I can cope. Naturopaths work along similar lines, where they treat many illnesses through diet and exercise. You may not be actually ill, but since becoming unemployed you may well feel below par. You don't seem to have the energy you had before. You skin looks a bit slack and grey. Your hair doesn't seem to have the body or shine it once had. You may look as though you need a good night's sleep, even though you're sleeping longer than normal. You generally feel in need of a good tonic.

It can soon become a vicious circle. When you feel low, you are less able to summon the energies needed to start making any improvements to yourself or your life. And when the job interview eventually happens, you turn up so eager to make a good impression, but looking as if you could already do with a few weeks' holiday. Yet when you are making progress, your sense of well-being inevitably improves. You look vibrant somehow; life and health seem to shine from you.

Being without work is no easy business. You may no longer have your boss breathing down your neck, but there is certainly plenty to worry about. With all the new sorts of problems you are having to deal with, and which may continue for at least the next few months, you need to be in top form. You need to look one hundred per cent fit and healthy for when you are called for that vital interview, or when you make that appointment about a loan for your new business idea. It is a challenge to stay on top when unemployed, and you need to be A1 in order to make sure you get the best out of it instead of going under.

But how do you get going in the first place?

It may be a good idea to first of all think about the last chapter. Are you sure you aren't hanging on to old grievances; do you perhaps feel that you need to talk through some of your current worries; does your mind feel more like a hamster in a wheel than a cool, tranquil pond? It might be best to address any underlying issues as well as simply looking for the answer to well-being from external sources. You might also like to refresh your memory about self-development (see Chapter 6).

There is a tendency when you are out of work to over-indulge. You may want to drink more than normal, smoke or eat more. It's understandable. You need to find comfort during these difficult times, and these are perhaps the most accessible and seemingly satisfying sources. They help to ease the pain, hurt and frustration you may be feeling and give at least some sense of enjoyment. In moderation there is no problem, but if they become over-used they will obviously lead to difficulties, and add to existing ones. The bank balance may start to feel the pinch even more because of your over-indulgences, and the temporary highs leave an even lower low in terms of feeling worse, health-wise.

It may also be that if you have been feeling depressed, this is reflected in your body, too. Your system may have become more sluggish and you may have started to put on weight. Seeing your looks deteriorate only makes you feel even more depressed. So check out your emotional health first of all.

▪ FOOD

What you eat is vitally important in helping you feel more on top of things and able to cope. You may have fallen into the habit of 'not being bothered' about the meals you throw together, or you might even find yourself living on snack-type meals every few hours, simply because doing so relieves the boredom of sitting around all day. Having an enjoyable programme of activities is just as important for your physical health as it is for your mental well-being.

Healthy eating needn't mean expensive eating; in fact it is probably quite the opposite. You won't have much money to spare for fattening nibbles, chocolates, sweets, cakes and biscuits; or for eating rich foods in expensive restaurants. Instead, you now have the opportunity to give your diet a good overhaul and boost. Eating well will reflect itself in how you look and how you feel. And it is important that you *do* eat well. It is an indication that you feel yourself worthy to be looked after. It shows how much you care about yourself, and you do care, don't you? Stuffing it full of poor-quality food isn't the best way of showing it. Give it good foods so that it can do its job properly, and as a result it will reward you by making you feel better.

Making sure that you do eat well needs an element of planning. Consider what foods you have available if you are growing your own and what fruits and vegetables are in season to help you decide what meals to make. Think about whether you could eliminate meat from your diet, which is not only expensive but also has a high fat content. Do some research into finding interesting recipes which use beans, pulses and lentils instead. If you can't bear the thought of cutting meat out altogether, use smaller amounts and make it go further by the addition in casseroles of beans or barley. Plan your weekly menus so that they make full use of everything you buy. For example, the water you cook your vegetables in can be saved and used as a base for a nourishing soup for next day's lunchtime meal. Aim to eat lots of the 'filler' foods like wholemeal bread, potatoes, pasta and rice. Eat plenty of whatever cheap vegetables are in season, including any sprouting vegetables for stir-fries or salads. Limit the amount of fats and fatty foods you eat, as well as cakes, biscuits and puddings. Eat fruit for dessert instead, perhaps from your store of produce you have bottled along with some home-made yoghurt. Save processed foods for special treats.

Eating a wholefood diet (one which restricts any processed

foods) is perhaps the best way to make sure you are eating healthily. You might also find that in the process you trim down if you have been putting on weight. Your system will feel less sluggish and in turn you will feel more energetic because your body will be getting the nutrients it needs. When under stress our bodies quickly use up supplies of vitamins B and C in particular, so it is important that you do eat healthily to ensure you are getting enough of those vital elements. Failure to do so will mean your body ends up trying to run effectively on only two-star fuel.

The way you cook food can also affect its quality — and cost you unnecessary fuel bills. Instead of over-cooking vegetables in lots of water, buy a steamer which allows more than one vegetable to be cooked in the same pan with only about an inch of water. Stir-frying is a quick and nutritious way to cook both meat and vegetables. You might also like to think about including the occasional day eating only raw foods. There has been lots of publicity over the years about how good it is for you — and it saves on cooking bills.

▪ EXERCISE

Desirable though you may think having a job is, it can be less than beneficial for your health in terms of the amount of exercise you get. Even so, you may be thinking that it's probably more than you're getting at the present moment in your new career as couch potato. Now you have the opportunity, along with healthy eating, to turn around your fitness profile. If going up stairs leaves you gasping for breath, now is definitely the time to think about getting fitter. And the circumstances couldn't be better.

Since saving money is high on your list of priorities, you can take advantage of the opportunity to cut costs and increase your exercise by nothing simpler than walking whenever you have the chance. Petrol money and bus fares can be saved, and you will be helping yourself get fitter into the bargain. You could also think of joining the local branch of the Ramblers' Association; your library or Citizens Advice Bureau should have the address of your local branch. If there isn't one you could contact the headquarters and offer to set one up. If that seems too formal for you yet you would like to walk with a group, see if you can get some friends or neighbours interested. You could advertise for people on the community noticeboard, at the drop-in centre or on your library's noticeboard. Getting together with others in a shared activity can be lots of fun, and also helps to maintain commitment. It's too easy to cry off from going on a short hike if it's just you and the thermos, but more difficult if you know that three or four others will be standing on the corner waiting for you.

Ramblers' Association
1/5 Wandsworth Road
London SW8 2LN
Tel. 071 582 6878

If you have a bike, or can borrow one, cycling is another alternative. It's cheap, gets you there faster than walking and helps keep you fit. Similarly there may be a local cycling group you could join, or you might like to set up one of your own. Planning an interesting route for a day's run around can be much more fun if there's a group of you.

Still using your own resources, now might be the time to think about doing what just about everyone else seems to get around doing at some stage or other: jogging. You may already have a good pair of running shoes but if not, try to run on grass to reduce the impact on your joints. Start off slowly, perhaps by jogging at a comfortable pace for the distance between two lamp posts and walking the distance between the next two. Gradually build up over a space of time. There's little to be gained by frightening your muscles with a four hundred yard dash when you haven't moved quicker than a snail for longer than you care to remember. Apparently you should aim to increase your heart and breathing rate, but not so that it leaves you breathless. As with all exercise, do check yourself out with your GP first if you haven't been active for some time. You don't want to end up damaging yourself; the aim is to get fitter!

There may also be a local running track you could use. Phone the leisure and recreation department at the town hall to ask for details. You could do what a local group near me did and set up a women's (or men's) jogging group. As with all groups it will help keep the commitment and motivation alive.

On a more formal basis, you might like to think about joining an exercise class. There may be concessionary rates at your local sports centre or adult education college. Have a look at what's available in your area. Now might be the chance you have been waiting for to have a go at yoga, t'ai chi, basketball or table tennis. Your local swimming pool may also have a range of classes, or you might simply want to include a swim in your new weekly schedule. There is also the additional benefit of increasing your social contacts; so important when you are out of work. But if you feel shy about publicly flaunting your lack of fitness, there are plenty of exercises you can do in the privacy of your own home. The topical step routines can be done on the bottom step of a flight of stairs, on an upturned speaker or on a secured pile of telephone directories. Gentler exercise routines which rely more on stretching and increasing suppleness could be more your scene. There are lots of books currently available for you to follow. Go to your public library and find out what's on offer.

If individual exercise isn't really your thing, then team sports might be. Find out if there is a local team you could join: football (men's and women's), rugby (men's and women's), rounders, netball, basketball, five-a-side, baseball, to name a few. And if there isn't one going for the sport you're interested in, you know what to do — start your own. You could even start a league table going and establish a cup final to give the teams something to aim for at the end of the year. Team building not only has lots of potential benefits for you in social terms, it is also a very marketable skill which could be included on your CV.

Just being out and about in the great wide open helps free the mind and make you feel better. Include as many outdoor activities as possible into your new schedule. Sitting indoors all day will make your system become sluggish — and it will soon start to show. You will also be cutting down on the amount of necessary sunlight our bodies need to manufacture vitamin D. Lack of sunlight quite badly affects some people, who become severely depressed, developing what has been called Seasonal Affective Disorder. While you may not be as sensitive as this, we all need to feel the sunlight and breathe fresh air. You could offer to dig someone's garden, do their market shopping for them, or take the dogs for a walk. Not only will you be helping them, you will also be getting the benefit of being out of doors, even if it is only for a short while. It may also give you some ideas for a mini-enterprise, such as setting up in business as a regular day-time dog-walker for people who leave their dogs at home most of the day.

▪ STAYING WELL

Although we tend to think of exercise as necessary to maintain good health, we tend to forget that relaxation is also important, especially if you are feeling under a lot of strain. Learning how to relax can positively help you cope better with life's day to day problems. See if there is a local relaxation class you could join. Ask your GP if there doesn't seem to be one available through your local sports provision. S/he may be able to recommend a local group run by a health education or other group.

Learning how to meditate can also be very beneficial and is a useful skill to have. When I want to meditate I do a pile of ironing. Yes, seriously. I turn on my favourite music and with either a glass of wine to hand or a good cup of tea I drift away while the iron glides silently backwards and forwards. It may not be the conventional way, but it certainly works for me. Try to find ways which help you switch off in this way. Water therapy seems to work well with some people (otherwise known as washing up!). See also page 130.

There are also a range of therapies which can help restore both physical and mental well-being and which you might like to investigate. Although some therapies have to be carried out by professionals and can be expensive, there are others which are safe to perform as self-therapy and some which are specifically designed for it. You could investigate: pressure-point massage, Bach flower remedies, aromatherapy, herbal treatments, crystal therapy, colour therapy. Go to your local library and see what books they have available on any of the above. Health food shops often have books for sale which you could usefully browse through to give you some ideas. And who knows, it may lead on to more than just a passing interest and provide a way into self-employment.

Achieving and maintaining good health can be difficult to focus on when you're busy holding down a full-time job, doing justice to family life and keeping the social side going. At present you have the opportunity to perhaps redress some of the imbalances which have crept into your lifestyle over the years. This isn't something to do just while you're out of work. You could think of it as a re-education programme and an investment in yourself which you can carry forward with you into your future, regardless of whether it is in employment or not. Learning to look after your body is another opportunity which being unemployed brings to you. Perhaps after years of misuse, now is the time to look seriously at how you might correct the balance, and in the process show to yourself and others how much you really care for and cherish yourself. If people can see you like yourself, they will magically be drawn to do the same — and one of them might be the person with a job to offer.

15 ▪ *Relationships*

Families. They can be a source of comfort, strength and joy — or they can be a pain in the proverbial. The same can be said of partners and friends.

While you were in work or otherwise engaged things seemed to tick over reasonably well. Partners met at the end of day, perhaps for only a short while before one or both went off again to follow up some other pursuit: doing the ironing, going for a drink, meeting up with friends, going out for the evening.

But now, as if things weren't feeling difficult enough, your closest relationships seem to be less a source of comfort and more like a thorn in the side. It all adds to the confusion. Your mind may be in an unsettled whirl as you come to terms with, and try to make sense of, what is happening to your life. You have a lot of important questions to ask yourself and even more important decisions to make, yet no one seems to understand. Instead, they simply seem to get on your nerves. So you find yourself with even more problems to deal with: your nearest and dearest.

▪ PARTNERS

Unemployment may be happening to you, but any partner who is sharing your life will also be feeling the fall-out from what is happening. They too may have felt in a state of shock and disbelief if you were made redundant without warning. They too may be struggling to try to come to terms with what has happened. Although it is you who is out of work, they too will be experiencing the consequences of a change in lifestyle, a reduced income and a change of plans. They may actually be feeling even more powerless than you, if they have relied on you as the main breadwinner. And so while you are crying out for comfort and support, they may be feeling that they need the same, too. Unfortunately, they may be wanting it from the one person who obviously won't feel able to give it: you. So you both end up wanting the same thing from each other and which neither has to give. Frustrations and resentments soon build up.

In an attempt to help, your partner may suggest possible jobs for you to do or places to apply. Unless they understand well what you are looking for, and the significance of your CV in relation to any job on offer, any suggestions may seem totally inappropriate, useless and even downright thoughtless. Being told to apply for the vacancy as a truck driver will not be appreciated if your last job was as transport manager. You may eventually choose to make that shift at a later date and in your own time, but having it suggested by someone else that you had better come down a peg or two since no one wants you for the job you did last, can come as a bitter insult. Even appropriate and helpful suggestions can feel like undue pressure is being put on. When you're feeling vulnerable and unsure of yourself while being unemployed it's easy to take suggestions as meaning 'Why don't you pull your finger out and get on with it,' or 'You just aren't doing enough to find a job.' And so the pressure grows.

Having daily schedules disrupted, however simple, can also take its toll, especially if your partner normally stays at home. It is quite common for them to consider the home their 'territory' while you are usually out doing the nine to five. To find another body encroaching on their own schedules and timetables can feel very threatening and frustrating. Just when they normally do the vacuuming, you settle yourself down to write some application letters. Thursday is the day they do their shopping, but now the money isn't available until Monday. And just having another body constantly around the home can be very irritating. Their personal and private time can feel invaded and they may feel cross with you, but not realize why.

On the other hand, your partner having a job may also bring difficulties. They come home tired from their day's work only to find you lounging around in your slippers and perhaps feeling a bit down about things. The frustrations and worries they have experienced through the day suddenly come flying out, directed at the sitting target — you. With little understanding it would be easy for them to feel aggrieved that while they are working their damnedest, you seem to spend your time reading newspapers and idling your time away. They may be feeling that you should be at least out on the streets, actually looking for a job there. And if they have to come home to start doing household chores, because that's the way things are done (well, you always used to come home much too late to cook dinner), eventually they are bound to want to vent their anger.

If they don't have a job already, your partner may decide to start applying too in order to help the financial situation. If they're successful, although it may mean the money worries recede a little, it can come as another blow to yourself. They have managed to do what you haven't yet been able to. They're successful — and you already know you aren't. Ouch! Another blow to the ego. Add another resentment point and you've nearly reached a full score.

And so as if the run-of-the-mill pressures weren't enough, you may also be experiencing relationship pressures. Arguments flare for no good reason. Stormy moods seem to come from nowhere. And as for your sex life . . . . Passion now seems to be reserved for fuelling arguments.

▪ CHILDREN

The natural reaction towards children is to keep them safe and out of harm's way. Because of this, it may appear to be the best option to keep them in the dark about what has happened if unemployment has suddenly struck. Children are highly sensitive and even though they may be very young, they will probably pick up on the change in atmosphere in the house. They will notice the anxious conversations between the grown-ups and feel very excluded if conversations suddenly stop when they walk in the room to join in.

In picking up on the unsettled atmosphere, children may start to play up at school if not at home. It is easy for them to feel neglected as parental attention focuses on more pressing and urgent problems than the small-fry issues they want to bring to the family's notice. Their questions go unanswered, are brushed aside, they are told to 'Go and play.' But like all children, they need that attention and if they don't get it after asking directly for it, they will find other more sneaky and perhaps troublesome ways in which to get it.

On the other hand, in trying to make children feel involved (especially older teenagers) they can feel that problems are being dumped on them, without them having the skills to cope. Or they might simply feel that they are somehow being blamed for how things are when you suddenly lose your temper with them unnecessarily. They may not be aware of the reasons behind their feelings of resentment and it may just come out in moodiness, withdrawal, tearfulness or arguments.

Money will inevitably be tight. Without understanding why, if children suddenly find they are being told they can't have the things they might have reasonably expected beforehand, they will obviously start to feel cross and that you are being unfair. They may take it as a form of rejection; that you don't care. Tariq's parents are letting him go on the trip, why can't he go? Sue had a pair of new shoes for her birthday, why can't I? Answers of 'Because you can't,' or even 'Because we haven't the money,' may seem pretty feeble if they sense that last month it might have been different.

▪ PARENTS

You may still be trying to get your first job, and in the meantime are having to remain living in the family home. This was fine while you were at school, college or on a training course, but as you get older you may find that you are eager to be more independent. You want to be able to make, and live by, your own house rules instead of someone else's. You feel adult enough to make your own decisions, yet your parents may still see you as something of a child and start to interfere with what you do. You're eager to spread your wings, but are made to feel that you are being kept in a child-like state because of your financial dependency on them. Some parents may even like the fact that you are.

This can potentially be a very explosive situation. Parents may start to feel resentful that they are still having to support you, even though you are theoretically old enough to support yourself. This may be even more pronounced if your parents are out of work, too.

Some of what happens between partners may be similar to what happens between you and your parents. They look at you and only see you lounging around indoors, or hanging around with friends and doing nothing much. If it has gone on for a long time they may see your lack of success at finding work as a lack of trying, or even plain laziness. Without understanding your feelings and of how you are struggling to cope, they will have little empathy with your feelings of how futile any efforts are. Helpful suggestions are met with derision or scorn by you. You may feel that you just want to be left alone.

▪ FRIENDS

It is true that in going through difficult times you soon find out who your friends are. Unfortunately that is exactly the time when you could least do with finding out such a thing. Friends can be the one stable element in your life when all else seems to be suddenly thrown into confusion. Unfortunately they too can become part of that confusion. They may react in ways which you hadn't expected; some of this may be quite hurtful. In particular you may get the impression that friends from your previous workplace want to put a distance between you and them. This only adds to your feelings of rejection from the job. On the other hand it may be you who no longer feels able to face people who are still working in the place you are now excluded from. You may have conflicting feelings; you want to see the person, yet aren't able to feel comfortable with the connection they still have, and listen to all the stories they will want to tell you about the recent goings on. The rejection may come from you, not them.

We all need to off-load our problems and talk them through with someone. It may seem more appealing to do this with friends rather than family who can feel too close for comfort. The danger is that friends may be unable or simply not want to cope with your tales of woe after the first few times of telling. No one likes to feel that they are only serving as a convenient dump for others' troubles.

If they are unemployed as well, the situation might be different. You will have a common bond and a shared understanding of the difficulties you are going through. This can be a great support and help. However, things may not go quite so well if the other person gets a job. Although you may initially feel pleased for them, you may also feel that it accentuates your lack of success. With luck the friendship will survive this change, but you may find new practicalities interfere, not least of which is money.

Friends who are in employment, and in particular those who have never been out of work themselves, may have scarce understanding of how little spare cash there is available to go socializing. Eventually people just stop asking when they know that your likely response is, 'No, I can't really afford it,' or 'I'm waiting for my giro,' or some other phrase which basically says the same thing. It's a rejection whichever way one looks at it, and no one likes to put themselves in a position where they will keep getting more. So unfortunately your circle of friends may diminish even further, just when you feel you need them most.

▪ IMPROVING THE SITUATION

Problems, problems, problems. You feel you have more than your fair share to deal with, and now you find your relationships are causing even more. It might be tempting to bottle up your resentments and feelings in a vain attempt to keep the boat steady, but this rarely works. What tends to happen when you do this is that suddenly there's a flash flood when things become just too much, and there you are, capsized and even more confused and hurt.

The best way forward is to talk. This may sound simple, but it can be very difficult to do. It may mean opening up to someone; it may mean opening a can of worms. Keeping quiet and ignoring your feelings may seem a much more preferable option. But it's important how you are feeling about what's happening to you; about how you feel other people are treating you; about the messages you feel you are getting from them. Feelings and emotions need to be expressed and experienced — that's what they're there for, not to be repressed and ignored; in that way they cause trouble. Not talking about how you feel can also add to feelings of isolation.

'But I've tried talking to X about how I feel and now they just don't seem to want to know.' In talking to people about our problems, there is a danger that we unwittingly abuse their good will. If it seems to them that our needle is stuck as we whine on and on, going over the same ground again, it is understandable that they will begin to feel irritated or bored. Friends who are feeling like this are unlikely to want to bring it out into the open themselves, for fear of offending you — and yet the resentments are there. So, it is up to you. If you feel that things aren't quite right between you and your partner, parents or friends you must try to address the issue openly. It's best to set aside a special time to broach any difficult topics. Don't wait until you are in the middle of yet another argument to try and calmly talk things through. Pre-empt the situation, take control and open things up. If you feel confused by the other person's irritation, ask them about it.

If you reckon you have been less than honest about how you have been feeling, talk about it. If you feel your needs aren't being met, express them. If you feel people close to you are being too demanding, pressurizing or inconsiderate, let them know how you feel in a non-accusatory way.

By letting people know how you feel you can open up to a more honest day-to-day dialogue and should reach a better understanding between you. You give others a chance if you let them know where you're coming from; otherwise they will simply put the barricades up to any useful discussion. In being human we all have our shadow sides and being unemployed might be giving you and others the opportunity to get to know yours. This other side isn't evil, or something to be ashamed of; it is part of who we are. It only causes problems if it is ignored, when it will swell up to ugly proportions behind the scenes and really start making trouble. But give it a voice and help to integrate it into who you are and the little fellow becomes meek and mild again.

With children especially it is important for them to know what is happening on a practical as well as personal level. Use language which is appropriate to their age and explain the situation. This will help them to understand the 'why' behind why they can't do or have a lot of things that others can. It may still be hard for them, but at least they will have a better understanding. Give them lots of reassurances, cuddles and love to help them see that it is no reflection on how you feel about them.

Letting children know how you feel is also important; not so that you dump all your grievances on them, which is unfair and unrealistic to expect them to cope with, but just to let them know why you are acting the way you are. Without knowing you feel down in the dumps today because you've had another rejection letter, children may take your withdrawal as a personal slight against them. They may feel they have done something wrong and that they're not loved any more. Keep them in the picture and you save them from the agonies over misunderstanding your words and gestures. Come to think of it, this goes for everyone and not just children.

Once you start really talking you move towards reaching a better understanding and making better agreements. If your partner's irritation has been around having to do chores after a day's work, you could reach an agreement about what role s/he would like you to play. If your parents have been coming down heavy on the rules, you might discuss ways in which to make the situation more workable for all of you. If friends have been distant because you can't join in with their (expensive) activities, agree to plan alternatives which don't cost so much. If everyone is telling you to lighten up about your problems, your agreement might help you realize how heavy you have been with them.

Once this stage has been reached you are at a point where you can transform the difficulties into workable solutions. Together you can plan alternative ways of living and being together which enrich rather than erode the basis of your relationship. Travelling through difficult periods in your life is a journey towards a deeper understanding of yourself and others. This is not an opportunity to be missed.

▪ WHAT TO DO TO HELP

If you're not the person who is unemployed, you may be wondering what you can do to help. Perhaps you can see the person is in difficulties yet you're not sure about the best way forward. Keeping those lines of communication open is perhaps the best single thing you can do; encourage them to talk about their feelings and worries. You need not feel that you must have the answers for them and in turn feel worried that you don't. Just listening attentively to what they have to say, without judgment, is probably all it needs. The answers are for *them* to find; you can help by providing them with an opportunity to express how they feel.

You may find the following helpful, depending on the nature of your relationship with the person who is unemployed:

- If they seem to have lost the initiative, encourage them to set simple, daily targets which they can attain, such as going to the library to look at the papers or going to check on one or two noticeboards to see what is happening locally.
- Encourage them to see the positive in both themselves and the situation they are in.
- Don't deny their feelings when they say they are feeling down, by retorting with a 'Pull yourself together' attitude. Listen to what they have to say, try to understand what they are experiencing and ask them about what they would like to do to change it.
- Inventory the things you enjoy doing together (and which don't cost money).
- Reassure them of your feelings towards them.
- Make sure both you and they eat properly (Chapter 14).
- Make time for yourself and see to your own needs.
- Occasionally give them a simple treat. It needn't . be anything which costs money. A spontaneous hug or a single flower from the garden will do. It reassures them of your feelings towards them and reminds them that they are of some worth.
- If you feel you can't cope, get some help from outside. Contact your local branch of Relate (previously the Marriage Guidance Council; address in the telephone book), talk to a sympathetic family member from outside the home, a community leader or your GP. You need support through this difficult time too, and you need to establish your own support network. There may be a local group for partners of people who are unemployed, and if there isn't why not start one?
- If appropriate, suggest sources of help and support for the person who is unemployed. There may be a drop-in centre for people without work, a local self-help group, and again local sources, such as community workers, religious leaders, or others working in pastoral or community roles, may be able to offer help.

Being unemployed is difficult in itself, but with strong, supportive relationships it can be made much easier. Whenever we approach difficulties in our lives, we are being given the chance to grow even more as human beings. It is up to us to meet that challenge.

On your own. Whilst in a job, the words may have held the spirit of independence; of a soul successfully making its free way in the world, unfettered. Now as someone who is unemployed the words may have a different ring to them. They may speak to you with echoes of isolation; almost an outcast from welcome society. The other side of the coin seems to swivel into view and glint sharply at you.

Living on your own, either through choice or by circumstance, and being without work can present its own set of difficulties. You have the 'regular' ones of coping with the new situation and perhaps dealing with particular problems like debt. You may also feel you have another set of difficulties because you are on your own.

It may seem to you that others who have a family or who are in a relationship have the benefit of someone else being there. This may not have been an issue for you while you were in a job. Going out to work would have provided you with the important daily contact with other people which we all need, and close friends would have filled the more important points in your life. Occasional lovers would have given added highlights. But now it may feel that your only regular contacts are limited to the person behind the screen at the Unemployment Benefit Office and another person behind a different screen when you cash your giro cheque.

Friends may still be about, but if they had previously centred around work you may find it difficult to keep in contact with them. It can feel that a chasm has opened up which suddenly separates you, The Unemployed, from friends who form part of The Employed élite. Sometimes (but not always) the labels come first, and friendship second. Trying to keep in sight the person beneath the job title can be difficult for everyone, although in good friendships it doesn't matter. This can be an unpleasant thing to have to find out, perhaps about yourself as much as about your work-based friends. And even for those friendships which do survive, the established ground-rules no longer apply: inviting each other over to join dinner parties, buying each other lunch, spending evenings at your favourite bar, days at the health club, weekends away. With a reduced income, such luxurious entertainment quickly slips out of reach. Offers of 'I'll treat you; don't worry about paying' may be well meant, but can be difficult for your pride to accept if you're used to paying your own way. Knowing you can't return the gesture makes you think twice before accepting. Without working at the friendship to find new common ground, it may run the risk of faltering.

Having the regular routine of going out into the world on a daily basis when you're in work, provides us with lots of convenient reasons 'why': why we need to look presentable; why we need to look after ourselves; why we need to stay fit; why we need to keep our personal problems in perspective; why we get up in the mornings. Work provides everyone with the very convenient reason why. The challenge which presents itself now is to find another reason to keep yourself looking well; another one to get up in the morning. Work isn't the only reason to life, and you now have the opportunity to find out what the others are and to find ones which are less dependent on outside changeable forces like employers.

It has to be said that with family around it is much easier. They tend to nudge reminders to you if they think you might be letting things slip too far. It's like having a sort of personal barometer which taps you instead of the other way round. When you're on your own the only reading you get is from yourself. Changing to more casual clothes can turn into looking sloppy; not bothering to style your hair might lead to letting it go a day too long without washing; a more flexible daily routine may lead to day-long snacking, late nights and long lie-ins; no longer having the funds to go to health clubs seems to become a reason not to bother exercising at all. With only yourself to justify your actions it's easy to bypass noticing just what sort of a job you are making of looking after yourself.

Besides reflecting our outer images, other people also serve to show us when we might be getting things out of perspective, or if we are becoming too wrapped up in our problems. It's easy for anyone to do this who is unemployed, regardless of whether they are on their own or not. When unemployment happens to you, it feels like the gravity of the situation is yours alone. Trying to find the new job, a way through, a new answer, makes us turn inward and focus on what's going on in our minds to such an extent it can come to feel like an out-of-control carousel, with your thoughts forever jumping up and down in turn like those gaudy fun-fair horses. We become almost mesmerized as they flash on and off, round and round, one after the other. Worry can seem like a constant companion where friends may previously have come in and nudged it out of the limelight.

Others may help you keep a sense of perspective; rightly or wrongly they can also help to sound off against. You may well feel very angry about what has happened to you and want to lash out with frustration at what seem like new problems, obstacles and blockages. It's much easier to do when there's a sitting duck in the armchair opposite, who after you've ranted and raved also then conveniently props up your sagging ego when you're down; cheers you up; tells you it will be alright and makes you a cup of tea.

Of course all this is how we fantasize about how others would be acting in an ideal situation. The reality of having people constantly around us might be far from how we imagine it to be. Irritations, squabbles, misunderstandings, judgmental looks and words, accusations, unsympathetic remarks, the list is endless. What may have seemed like an ideal from the outside may be very different from the inside, except in a few cases. The stresses and strains of being without work affect not just the person who it is happening to, but also those within close range, too. So before you dream away into 'if only-s', remind yourself of what the true reality is probably like.

▪ ADVANTAGES

Despite how it may seem, there are many advantages to being on your own at this time. Perhaps the most obvious is that you will not be having to deal with fractious partners or family members who find outlets for their own anger and frustrations in petty arguments and unhelpful behaviour. You're already at an advantage. And because there is just you, there are fewer feelings of responsibility towards other adults. Instead of feeling you have to carry various others, or that they are dependent on your next success or failure, and that you have to see to their needs, you are in a much better position to focus your energies on yourself. Other people with families may be under pressure for financial or other reasons simply to get any job which is on offer. You are in the enviable position of being able to take your time over your decisions without the risk of upsetting anyone else or clashing with their aims.

It may be that you decide that now really is a good time to take a breather from work for a little while in order to give you time to reassess. You may want to take the opportunity to have a good long look at where you are in your career and what this enforced break's message may be. You may even want to take time out for yourself, something which you may not have been able to do for a long time while you've been coping with the responsibilities of work. You can do all this without having anyone on your back, as partners or well-meaning family members might be.

As a result of your investigations you may decide that a complete change of direction and even lifestyle is in order. Seizing the chance to reach a breakthrough towards realizing your true life aims is so much easier when you don't have others' domestic baggage to negotiate around. If you decide that what you should really be doing is missionary work in some far-flung continent or that you should return to your childhood ambition of being a writer/artist/musician/doctor, you can do it. You know what the consequences are for your own life and can work with them, but trying to combine your heart's desire with the conflicting demands of somebody else's can be difficult and compromises may have to be sought. If you want to go and 'do your own thing', however radical, it is much easier when you're on your own.

It is also a lot easier to adapt your lifestyle to take into account your reduced income. You might decide that now is as good a time as ever to lose a bit of weight and go on a diet. If you wanted to try fasting before, you now have the chance to try it out. Switching your diet over to one which takes into account your purse as well as your health is simple to do when you're on your own, but can cause mutinous disruptions in a meat-eating, biscuit-addicted, hamburger-and-fries household. You want to eat healthily — you eat healthily; you want to go vegetarian — you do it; you want to crunch your way through raw foods and salads — go ahead. Life can be so much simpler on your own.

The same can be said of establishing new workable routines. Less flexible and adaptable people can be thrown into states of great agitation if late-evening snacks are cut out or bedtimes are brought more in line with heating economies. Battling against those who believe household rituals are writ large and in stone can make life so difficult. Thank goodness you don't have to contend with those sorts of problems. You can mix and match according to what suits you and what you would like to try out. Some of the chapters in the book may have given you ideas about new areas and possibilities to investigate. Once you have decided, you can go ahead instead of having to cope with the doubt and wet-blanket approach of others who try to put dampers on fledgling plans. If you want to do it — do it.

▪ STRATEGIES

Although the benefits of being on your own are indeed many, they may still leave gaps in the provision, as it were. Yes, you still want a shoulder to cry on every now and again; you want your ego bolstering up; you need to let out your confusion of feelings and worries. Thankfully you can plan your strategies to ensure your needs are met.

Within families, it is easy to assume that the other person is the one who should carry your burdens with you. Without thinking, they are taken as a convenient dumping ground for all your woes and inevitably this can lead to resentments. In your position, you still have the need to unburden just like everyone else, but fortunately you run less of a risk of alienating just one individual, so long as you are careful. With close friends it is easier to accept when they draw the line if it seems you are taking them for granted; with awareness on your part it won't even get to that stage. Because friends at the end of the day walk out of the door and back to their own lives, you are reminded that they have their own things to be getting on with. When you meet they will want to tell you their own stories about what has been happening, share with you their worries and ask you for your advice about what they should do. It is less easy to take advantage of others.

Friends should still be there for you though. If you feel they aren't then it's up to you to broach the issue. It may be that they feel a bit out of their depth in coping with your emotional outbursts, or your need for consolation. They may need reassurance from you as to what you want from them eg someone just to hear you out every now and then, not to provide answers. As was mentioned in the previous chapter, if some of your relationships seem to be running into difficulties, you may have to take the initiative and open a discussion about what is troubling you, or what you think is troubling them. Entering difficult stages in a relationship is often an opening towards reaching a greater level of understanding and appreciation of each other.

On the other hand, it may be that you feel that your needs aren't being met, yet you don't know why. Reflect on what it is you're actually wanting from someone. Now think about whether you have let that person know what it is you do want. It may be glaringly obvious to you, but others may not be as sensitive as you, and nor may they be mind-readers! Without knowing what you need, you give others little chance of coming up with the goods for you. But with the right messages and the right information, they would probably be only too willing to do what they can to help.

Support from friends and family members is important, but because they are a little bit more removed from you, you may need to help them help you. And if you should start to run into difficulties, keep those lines of communication open and talk out your worries and concerns about what is happening to your relationship with them. It may turn out that you simply need to find new scenarios in which you can socialize on a more equal footing. Expensive dinners with all the trimmings may be out, but meeting up for long walks in the park and then a hot cup of chocolate in a cafe afterwards may be just as enjoyable for both of you, if not more so. But without talking you will never be able to find a satisfactory answer.

You won't want to dump on your friends or family all the time so you may need to find alternative ways of expressing your feelings. Because you have the luxury of having the time and space to yourself, you can try out different ways to do this. You may want to release feelings of anger in a physical way: lying on the bed and beating the mattress with your arms and legs; punching pillows or cushions; throwing a few choice objects across the room or kicking some others down the stairs (non-breakable if you don't fancy clearing up afterwards). Shrieking, bellowing and screaming into pillows is a good way to release as well. You could also try the empty chair approach if there are specific people you feel angry with: sit in front of an empty chair and talk to it as though the person you're angry with is in it; change places and sit in the empty chair and answer all the accusations and angry words as if you were the person you're actually angry with. Try a few different methods of releasing pent-up emotions and see which ones help most.

On a more creative level, you could consider channelling your anger and frustrations into something more constructive. There is a lot of energy generated by these emotions, and you may want to mobilize it to help you get a special project off the ground. For example, if you feel aggrieved at how people who are unemployed are treated you could form an action group to try to do something constructive about redressing the balance; or you may want to channel it into political activity at either the local or national party level. Think about ways in which you could use the vast amount of energy which these sorts of emotions put at your disposal.

In other creative ways, you could use different media to provide a way to open up to and express how you're feeling. When you are on your own you can wave your paintbrush enthusiastically over a piece of paper or canvas to your utter and glorious satisfaction without someone leering over your shoulder and passing unhelpful comments like 'Not quite a Picasso, is it?' Similarly with writing, music, singing; they are all outlets for expressions of what we are feeling within. And along with the satisfaction gained from opening ourselves up in this way and letting it all out, there is also the pleasure we receive from the pursuit itself: experimenting with different methods can be lots of fun.

It will also help to have a daily schedule and an on-going diary of events to work to. Without the formal structure of the working week to operate around, time can hang heavy on your hands, and even more so without the daily input and distractions from others. Chapter 9 may have given you some ideas about different ways in which to get out and about, as may some of the other chapters, too. Meeting new people and becoming part of new and different structures provides opportunities for creating valuable support networks. Friends may not provide all that you need right now, and it is perhaps unfair to expect them to, so looking for alternatives to supplement what they *can* offer is an important step to take.

You might also like to investigate what is available in terms of more formal support networks in your area. Many are suggested in the previous chapter, including where to go if things really start to get on top of you. With an enjoyable new schedule created, the support of available friends and by developing a few coping strategies of your own, any difficult times can be worked through with greater ease.

It may seem to some that living on your own through a period of unemployment is unthinkable, yet it offers significantly more opportunities to develop an infinitely rewarding lifestyle, one which is totally in tune with helping you discover your self and your life's true aims.

17 ▪ *Summary*

'Life without work' can sound like a prison sentence, reflecting how unemployment is perceived and experienced by some people. If this is how you initially interpreted it, hopefully the book will by now have given you some alternatives to consider and begun to fill your head with the many possibilities which do exist.

After the initial shock of finding yourself out of a job has worn off, or after the second wave of possible despair at the length of time you have been unemployed has passed by, you may be in a better position to appreciate some of the positive aspects of this time in your life. It isn't an easy time, but it may be the only one in which you have the opportunity to explore all those other options in life, ones which the nine-to-five regime keeps firmly on the sidelines; ones which may lead to an infinitely more rewarding life.

Although it may seem that your horizons have shrunk, it is a time in which surprisingly they can also expand; perhaps not in the same direction you were heading before, but into newer, unexplored territories. You have the chance to discover what opportunities have been lying in wait during this special time while you are not restricted by time-consuming, money-chasing and status-seeking jobs.

I hope the book has given you a clue about ways in which to help yourself, which paradoxically can come about by helping others. Normally this is left to the remote and de-personalized action of signing cheque books when we know we have the cash to spare but no time for real involvement. Money is useful and may buy an elderly person a new pair of gloves, but I feel sure they would much rather have someone to hold their hand instead over a friendly chat and cup of tea, so that their hearts are warmed as well as their hands.

I hope too that the book has helped you to start realizing

your own sense of power over the situation in which you find yourself. Sharing that power, and banding together with like-minded others may be how you see the best way forward, keeping the reins in your own hands instead of waiting for be-suited others to provide what they think you need. You may need to find courage and bravery to go into what may be uncharted seas and no book can give you that. But if your aims are true, and they serve higher ideals than just a quick buck in your pocket, you will receive all the help and support you need to enable you bravely to steer your way through.

Besides work and money, optimism is the main thing which is in short supply through times of recession. Without it, the future looks bleak even at the best of times. If the book has sparked just one iota of optimism, then this may be enough to fuel your own ideas and spur you into action.

It may be difficult to appreciate at first, but perhaps you are now in a good position to consider what a wonderful chance we are given through unemployment. A chance to transform the meaning of the title from a life sentence to a life affirmation. There is indeed *Life Without Work*.

▪ Further Reading

Chapter 1, pp.9–18

What Colour Is Your Parachute, Richard Nelson Bolles (Ten Speed Press, UK Edition, 1993)

Putting Redundancy Behind You, Sheila Cane and Peter Lowman (Kogan Page, 1993)

Changing Course – A Positive Approach to a New Job or Lifestyle, Maggie Smith (Mercury 1992)

What Are You Doing With the Rest of Your Life? Choices in Mid-Life, Paula Payne Hardin (New World Library, 1992)

Chapter 2, pp.19–28

National Welfare Benefits Handbook, and the *Rights Guide to Non-Means-Tested Benefits*, both published yearly by the Child Poverty Action Group

Creating Abundance, Andrew Ferguson (Piatkus, 1993)

Chapter 3, pp.29–40

Go For It (Essential Guide to Opportunities for Young People), Martyn Lewis (Lennard Publishing 1993)

Career Opportunities for Anyone, Anne Purdon (CRAC 1991). For young people without qualifications.

How to Get a Job After 45, J. Bayley (*Daily Telegraph*/Kogan Page 1992)

Job-hunting Tips for the So-called Handicapped – or People Who Have Disabilities, Richard Nelson Bolles (Ten Speed Press 1991)

How to Write a Winning CV, Alan Jones (Century Business 1992)

Job Hunting Made Easy, John Bramham and David Cox (Kogan Page 1992)

How to be Headhunted Across Europe, Stephanie Jones and Yvonne Sarch (Macmillan Press 1993)

How to Start a New Career, Judith Johnstone (How to Books 1992)

How to Get a Job in Europe, Mark Hempshal (How to Books 1992)

Get That Job!, Clive Fletcher, (Thorsons 1992)

Chapter 5, pp.51–60

The Kogan Page Mature Student's Handbook, Margaret Korving (Kogan Page 1991)

CRAC Directory of Further Education 93/94 (Hobsons Publishing 1993)

CRAC Directory of Higher Education 93/94 (Hobsons Publishing 1993)

Chapter 6, pp.61–71

The Personal Growth Handbook, Liz Hodgkinson (Piatkus 1993)
Reclaim Your Power, Khaleghl Quinn (Thorsons 1991)
I Want to Change But I Don't Know How – A Step-by-step Programme for Mastering Your Life, Tom Rusk and Randy Read (Thorsons 1986)
Life Choices and Life Changes Through Imagework – The Art of Developing Personal Vision, Dina Glouberman (Mandala 1989)
Springboard – Women's Development Workbook, Liz Willis and Jenny Daisley (Hawthorn Press 1992)

Chapter 7, pp.72–84

Earning Money At Home, (Which? Books 1991)
How to Set Up and Run Your Own Business, (Daily Telegraph/Kogan Page 1993)
The publishers How to Books have a whole range on different aspects of self-employment, including How to Buy and Run a Shop and How to Start a Business From Home

Chapter 8, pp.85–94

The Complete Fundraising Handbook, Sam Clarke (Directory of Social Change, 1993)
A range of fundraising leaflets is available from Directory of Social Change (see p.000).

Chapter 10, pp.105–120

Self-Help Groups: Getting Started; Keeping Going, Judy Wilson (Longmans 1986)
Community Groups Handbook, Maggie Pearse and Jerry Smith (Journeyman, 1990). Can be ordered through Community Development Foundation (see page 80).

Chapter 12, pp.135–147

Complete Book of Self-Sufficiency, John Seymour (Dorling Kindersley 1992)
Running Your Own Smallholding, Richard and Pauline Brambrey (Kogan Page 1989)
How to Do Just About Everything (Reader's Digest 1990)
Household Hints and Handy Tips (Reader's Digest 1990)
501 DIY Supersavers – Hints and tips to save you time and money around the home, Pamela Donald (Piatkus 1991)

Cheaper and Better – Homemade alternatives to shop-bought products, Nancy Birnes (Optima 1988)

Chapter 13, pp.148–156

Self-therapy – A Guide to Becoming Your Own Therapist, Janette Rainwater (Aquarian Press 1989)
Change for the Better – A Life Changing, Self-help Psychotherapy Programme, Elizabeth Wilde McCormick (Unwin Paperbacks 1990)
Nutrition and Mental Health, Dr Carl Pfeiffer (Thorsons 1991)

Chapter 14, pp.157–165

The Whole Health Manual, Patrick Holford (Thorsons 1988)
The Ordinary Person's Guide to Extraordinary Health, Jillie Collings (Aurum Press 1993)
Endless Energy, Susannah and Leslie Kenton (Vermilion 1993)
Superliving, Peter Cox and Peggy Brusseau (Vermilion 1991)
Cheap and Easy, Rose Elliot (Fontana 1988). Recipe book.

Chapter 15, pp.166–176

Superlove, Anne Naylor (Thorsons 1993)
How to Love and Be Loved, Dr Paul Hauck (Sheldon Press 1983)
Making Marriage Work, Dr Paul Hauck (Sheldon Press 1981)
Loving Relationships – 2, Sondra Ray (Celestial Arts Publishing 1992)
The Relate Guide to Better Relationships, Sarah Litvinoff (Vermilion 1992)

Chapter 16, pp.177–185

Healing Your Aloneness, Erika J. Chopich and Margaret Paul (Thorsons 1990)
How to Be Your Own Best Friend, Dr Paul Hauck (Sheldon Press 1988)
Happy to be Single, Liz Hodgkinson (Thorsons 1993)

▪ Index

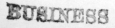